CW00733534

Constance Markievicz, Colette and Lou Andreas Salome shared a remarkable independence of mind. I chose to write about them not because they were famous, but because the life of each represents the difficult evolution of an identity formed by opposition, in defiance of the demands of society. Their steadfast visions of the world and their places in it gave them the strength to reject convention.

Constance was born into a wealthy Anglo-Irish Protestant family, landed gentry who had colonised Ireland centuries before. She became a leader of the Irish separatist movement and converted to Catholicism. The play is concerned with her transformation and the steps which took her from one side to the other. It leaves her when she is on the point of becoming an inspirational figure in the Easter uprising.

Colette came from a somewhat Bohemian lower middle-class family in provincial France. She began her literary career as an anonymous hack for her husband, when the family finances were at a low ebb. Divorced from him, she made her living as a music-hall performer. The subject of much scandal and gossip, she eventually settled into a respectable and respected old age and was given a state funeral – a rare honour for a woman.

Lou was a wealthy aristocrat of mixed European blood, brought up on the fringes of the Russian court. She could have made a brilliant marriage, but instead chose a life of scholarship with an academic husband. She studied with Freud and became one of the first psychoanalysts. However, she is best known for the effect she had on the philosopher, Nietzsche, and the poet, Rilke – being the pupil of the former and the mistress of the latter. She was truly self-possessed, resisting physical and mental domination by the powerful men who kept her company.

All these women had a strength of purpose which made public opinion irrelevant. They are powerful role-models.

S. Freeman

THREE REMARKABLE WOMEN:

Three Plays by Sandra Freeman

Temple House Books
Sussex, England

All rights whatsoever in these plays are strictly reserved. All applications for performance, including professional, amateur, motion pictures, recitation, lecturing, public reading, broadcasting, television and the rights of translation into foreign languages should be addressed to the Author, via the Publishers or to:

New Plays and Players Theatre Company
13 Walpole Terrace
Kemptown
Brighton
Sussex, BN2 2EB

This book is sold subject to the condition that it shall not, by way of trade or otherwise, be lent, re-sold, hired out, photocopied or held in any retrieval system or otherwise circulated without the publisher's prior consent in any form of binding or cover other than that in which this is published and without a similar condition including this condition being imposed on the subsequent purchaser.

Temple House Books
is an imprint of
The Book Guild Ltd.
25 High Street,
Lewes, Sussex

First published 1995
© Sandra Freeman 1995
Set in Times
Typesetting by Raven Typesetters, Chester

Printed in Great Britain by
Athenaeum Press Ltd,
Gateshead

A catalogue record for this book is
available from the British Library

ISBN 0 86332 993 4

This book is dedicated to Faith O'Reilly, with love and thanks.

CONSTANCE AND CASI

Characters in order of appearance

JANKO, *a servant*
CASIMIR, *a Polish Count*
CONSTANCE, *an Anglo-Irish Lady*
EVA, *Constance's sister*

This play is in two parts, with no subdivisions. I intend that all the characters apart from Eva stay on stage most of the time, moving backwards and forwards as required.

This play was first performed by the New Plays and Players Theatre Company at the University of Essex in June 1986, under the title *Constance, Casi and Cathleen*. It was directed by Roy Grant and the cast was as follows:

JANKO	Patrick Horne
CASIMIR	Anthony Wise
CONSTANCE	Christine Drummond
CATHLEEN NI HOULIHAN	Jean Trend
EVA	Carol Passmore

The character of Cathleen has since been written out, hence the change of title.

PART I PARIS 1899

When the lights go up CASIMIR *is standing centre stage. He is dressed exotically for a ball. Polka music is playing softly. He is surveying the scene. Downstage sits* JANKO. *He looks at the audience for a good long moment before speaking.*

JANKO   The trouble with Paris is the horses. (*Pause*) Well, that's one of the troubles. There aren't any. Not what you'd call horses. Not like back at home. There we have horses. There we ride – gallop, gallop for miles. Here ... (*He shrugs*) you've been in the Bois de Boulogne. You've seen what they call thoroughbreds trotting up and down tame as poodles! City animals, bred to show off their owners' clothes and figures. As for those broken-down wrecks they use to pull the cabs, well ... (*Gestures towards* CASI) he doesn't seem to mind. Rides a bike instead. I ask you! What am I supposed to do with a bike? That's the other thing. Half the time I've got nothing to do. He doesn't know how to keep me busy, especially with the life he leads. Bohemian artists don't usually have valets.

CASI   (*Meditatively*) My wife is dying. A long way from here. We were in love once. We were very very young. We are still young. I am sad for her but it is not my fault. And I am very much alive.

JANKO   Like now. Just hanging about. Waiting to see if he needs me. Can't even follow one of those little flower girls in case he comes out and can't find me.

CASI *comes downstage.*

CASI   Janko!

JANKO   (*To audience*) Hallo! A bit of action at last!

3

CASI	Janko, it's very boring in there.
JANKO	It's just a little bit boring out here.
CASI	Why don't you take me to where life is really going on, to where the people are?
JANKO	You think I know where that is?
CASI	Of course.
JANKO	How could I? I'm always where you are. Watching your lot go in and out.
CASI	I give you a night off every week. Then you go to places I don't know about.
JANKO	You're right!
CASI	Take me there.
JANKO	I don't know about that.
CASI	I need to look at beautiful women. I need to find models who will let me paint them in their natural loveliness, not in their diamonds and silks. Let's go. *Enter* CONSTANCE. *She too is extravagantly dressed, with a velvet fur-trimmed cloak thrown over her dress. She comes towards* CASI *and* JANKO, *gives a brilliant smile and moves upstage. Standing upstage,* CONSTANCE *removes her cloak to reveal her splendid costume.*
CASI	Wait here Janko, I think I'll go back inside.
JANKO	Yes sir. Of course sir. (*To audience*) Sod it! CASI *approaches* CONSTANCE, *who gives him another brilliant smile. He bows, clicks his heels.*
CASI	Count Casimir Markievicz, at your service, madam. Would you care to dance?
CONSTANCE	Constance Gore-Booth. Pleased to meet you, sir. *The dance music changes to a waltz.*
CONSTANCE	Thank you, I would love to dance. *They begin to waltz slowly.*
CONSTANCE	Are you Russian?
CASI	Polish. From the Ukraine, but not Russian. CONSTANCE *and* CASIMIR *stop dancing.* CASIMIR *stands back to look at her.*
CASI	My dear Miss Gore-Booth ...
CONSTANCE	Constance ...

4

CASI	My dear Constance, you are a magnificent sight. Such elegance! I would like to paint you.
CONSTANCE	My dear Casimir, I was about to say exactly the same thing.
CASI	You are a painter?
CONSTANCE	I'm learning to be one. I'm finishing my studies here. I think I am becoming a good painter. It's what I care about most passionately. This ring is a wedding ring. I'm married to art.
CASI	Are you alone in Paris?
CONSTANCE	(*Laughs*) Of course not, I have many friends. I live in a jolly boarding house in the Rue de Rivoli with lots of people I know.
CASI	I see. I would have been surprised if such a well-bred English girl had been let loose in this naughty city.
CONSTANCE	I'm not a girl, I'm over thirty. I do what I like. And I'm not English. (*She opens her purse*) This is my card. Will you come tomorrow afternoon for tea? Then I can draw you. You have a wonderful head. Quite beautiful. I generally prefer women models, I am very moved by women's gentle faces and their fragile bodies. You excite me though. (*She looks closely at his face*) Will you come?
CASI	(*Bows. Very amused*) Only one thing could stop me. I must warn you that I am fighting a duel tomorrow at dawn. An affair of honour. If I live I shall arrive on your doorstep at four o'clock precisely.
CONSTANCE	Oh how silly! Grown men to shoot at each other for hurt pride.
CASI	He insulted my country and my people. Besides we're not shooting. We use swords. I fence better than I shoot.
CONSTANCE	I shoot very well.
	She bends to pick up her cloak. CASIMIR *picks it up for her and places it around her shoulders.*
CASI	Leaving already?
CONSTANCE	(*Holds out her hand – he takes it, grasps it firmly*) Goodnight Casimir, until tomorrow.

5

	He kisses her hand, releases it. She walks away. He hesitates for a moment, then turns and walks away in a different direction.
JANKO	Not a thought for me of course, just like him. Forgotten I exist until he gets back and needs his boots pulled off. (*To audience*) Always the same. He'll wonder where I am when he gets home if I'm not there first. (*Pause*) I don't know about you but I get the impression that these two might be seeing a lot of each other!
	CONSTANCE *and* CASIMIR *move back downstage.* CASIMIR *sits and takes up a rather heroic pose.* CONSTANCE *stands drawing him.*
CONSTANCE	Just another minute or so. I haven't quite got you, I'm afraid, but it's always like that, don't you find? You need time to get used to a person. Don't argue, I'm just doing the mouth. Next time I'll do a full figure. There, you can move.
CASI	May I look?
CONSTANCE	(*Hands over the drawing*) The eyes are wrong. Not wide enough apart. I know.
CASI	May I draw you?
CONSTANCE	If you like. (*Hands him a pencil*)
CASI	I'd like you to remain standing. It will be very quick.
CONSTANCE	It doesn't matter. I can stand very still for a long time. Even as a child I was a good sitter.
CASI	I wasn't. Those terrible family portraits.
JANKO	(*To audience*) Oh yes, very boring, family portraits, don't you agree?
CASI	I like the way you stand. Energy at rest. A lot of energy, Constance, on the point of being released. The stillness of a wild animal poised for flight. A gazelle.
CONSTANCE	Are you a poet as well?
CASI	(*Shrugs*) I write a little.
CONSTANCE	Poems?
CASI	Sometimes. Mainly dialogues, little plays.
CONSTANCE	May I read them?

6

CASI	They're in Polish. I've tried writing a bit in French, but it's not the same.
CONSTANCE	I suppose a writer must speak with the language of his own people.
CASI	Oh, I agree, sometimes it's not easy to know who your own people are. I was brought up as a Russian, and I had a French governess, so I feel at home in Paris.
CONSTANCE	I don't feel at home here, but I feel free. When I studied art in London I had to have a chaperone. And I was old, it was only a couple of years ago. I love Paris, I hated London, although I was born there.
CASI	Where do you feel you belong then? Turn your head back to where it was, slightly to the left.
CONSTANCE	Ireland of course. Lissadell in County Sligo. It's a place of mountains, woods and sea. That's my home, my family's home for three hundred years.
CASI	But you were born in London.
CONSTANCE	An accident!
CASI	Drawing is no good for catching you. I need paint. There is a vibrancy you can only achieve with colour. (*Puts paper and pencil down*)
CONSTANCE	I'll come round to pose for you, if you like. Wearing whatever colours you want. I'll come round tomorrow, shall I?
JANKO	(*To audience*) Marvellous, isn't it? None of this 'Your place or mine?' No problem. He hasn't come across many like her before, I tell you. Same time, next day. She's inspecting his etchings. No, I mean it, she really is!
	CONSTANCE *and* CASIMIR *shift their positions on stage.* CONSTANCE *scrutinises what she sees around her very carefully.*
CONSTANCE	You're right, your paintings are much better than anything else. These prints are quite lifeless by comparison
CASI	(*Dryly*) Thank you for your honest opinion.
CONSTANCE	There's no point in false flattery.

7

CASI	No.
CONSTANCE	I'd like you to give me an honest appraisal of all my work some time.
CASI	All right.
CONSTANCE	Tomorrow?
	Pause.
CASI	Constance, are we beginning a relationship?
CONSTANCE	I don't know what you mean.
CASI	Yesterday, today, tomorrow. We only met two days ago. Don't you have other plans, other friends?
CONSTANCE	Of course. But I'll change them. They're not important.
CASI	I am important?
CONSTANCE	Yes. (*Pause*) I'm sorry, can't you manage tomorrow?
CASI	Would you sit down in that chair please? Put your hands in your lap. (*He crosses over to her, places her hands where he would like them, takes a few steps back, looks at her, shakes his head, goes over to her again, moves her hands, her head, steps back, nods*) Will that be all right?
CONSTANCE	Oh yes.
	CASIMIR *prepares himself to begin painting.*
CASI	I could manage tomorrow. It would be a little difficult, but I could. You see tomorrow is Thursday and Thursday afternoons and evenings I usually spend with the little lady who is good enough to pose for me on Thursday mornings.
CONSTANCE	The one in the painting with the beautiful breasts and the dark skin?
CASI	Exactly.
	Pause.
CONSTANCE	Well you'd better come to me the day after tomorrow then. (*Pause*) If that's convenient?
CASI	No it's not, but I will.
CONSTANCE	Don't put yourself to any trouble.
CASI	Keep your head quite still. Don't talk. I'll come because you intrigue me. I'll come because you are a beautiful woman and I find beautiful women difficult

8

to resist. What I want to capture is your passion. Don't blink, I'm working on the eyes. I want to see you on Friday. I would also like regular sittings for this portrait, once a week will do. I have commissions to work on meanwhile. And then I have my Thursdays, my precious Thursdays, when I feast my senses. You can blink now. You can even speak if you don't move your head. What should we do on Friday, Constance?

CONSTANCE   Can you be free on Saturday?

CASI   Instead of Friday?

CONSTANCE   As well as Friday.

CASI   You ask a lot.

CONSTANCE   I saw your bicycle in the hallway. Are you used to riding it far?

CASI   My dear, I have entered some of the most gruelling races in France.

CONSTANCE   Then let's cycle to Dieppe on Friday and back on Saturday.

CASI   Do you know how far that is?

CONSTANCE   (*Thinks for a second*) About seventy miles there and seventy miles back, I suppose. We'll start early in the morning if you think you can manage it. It would be fun!

JANKO   (*To audience*)Yes, it would. We haven't ridden as far as that for a few months. We'd usually expect to be in training. This is one occasion when he has to do without his gentleman's gentleman. Oh no, I don't cycle. I'll stay home and clean the silver.
CASIMIR *comes downstage limping and weary.*
CONSTANCE *remains upstage, stretching and bending.*

CASI   Janko we're ravenous. Here (*gives him some money*) Go and get us some bread, some cheese, some sausages and some beef. But bring us a glass of vodka first and some burgundy. (*To* CONSTANCE) You will love vodka!

CONSTANCE   I'd love a cup of tea.

9

CASI	You said you weren't English. (*To* JANKO) And some tea. Bring me the vodka before you make the tea. (*He goes back upstage*)
CONSTANCE	Casi, I'm sorry about last night. I did want to.
CASI	It was too soon. I knew it would be. I was very tired!
CONSTANCE	I haven't wanted to before. Thirty years old and never tempted. Isn't it extraordinary?
CASI	Not especially. Perhaps if you'd been a Catholic you would have become a nun. You would have married Christ, not Art.
CONSTANCE	Then I'm glad I'm a Protestant. Perhaps we could try again tonight.
CASI	When we've eaten we shall both fall so dead asleep we might not wake up for a week. (*Gently*) You hardly know me. You can't decide to give yourself to a strange man.
CONSTANCE	To you I thought I might. I trust you.
CASI	Oh my goodness!
CONSTANCE	It doesn't matter that you have mistresses.
CASI	Didn't your mother ever tell you to beware of handsome foreigners? That once they'd got what they wanted, they'd abandon you?
CONSTANCE	No. She had better things to talk about. What do you mean abandon me? How silly! I don't depend on you. I'd like you to be my friend, and I might as well lose my virginity to you because you're the most interesting man I've ever met. Good heavens, if you want to be with me, it surely can't be for the sake of my body. You have other women for that with full breasts and round thighs. (*She holds out her hand*) I like you a lot Count Casimir Markievicz. Will you be my comrade? CASIMIR *grasps her hand, automatically begins to raise it to his lips, sees her expression, and shakes it firmly.*
CASI	I would like that very much. JANKO *comes downstage*
JANKO	Here's your vodka. The tea will be a little while. In

10

	fact a long while, since I have got to go out and buy it. It's not something we have in stock, sir. If you remember, you've always said that drinking tea was a nasty Russian habit which as a resident of a piece of land stolen by Russia you were determined to resist.
CONSTANCE	Never mind. I'll have a glass of milk.
JANKO	You think we keep milk in the house?
CONSTANCE	I'll wait until we eat and just have a glass of wine.
CASI	You've opened several bottles?
JANKO	(*Scornfully*) Of course!
CONSTANCE	I can only drink a little.
JANKO	Don't worry madame, he can drink a lot!
	JANKO *moves away.*
CONSTANCE	Sit down and let me rub your calves.
	CASMIR *sits, she takes his shoes off and gently massages his feet and ankles and his calves.*
CONSTANCE	What hard muscles you have. I'm glad. Some men of your age are already soft. Then, they've done nothing to toughen them up. You've done so much, considering you're years younger than I am.
CASI	I never told you that!
CONSTANCE	Someone else did. Already kind friends have told me quite a lot. (*Pause*) About your marriage amongst other things.
CASI	I wasn't trying to deceive you. It didn't seem to matter.
CONSTANCE	It didn't. (*Pause*) I've done nothing yet. Oh, one or two small exhibitions, nothing really. You're known as a painter, you've got a wife and children.
CASI	That is what you call doing something?
CONSTANCE	Isn't it?
CASI	Perhaps, I don't know.
CONSTANCE	There are many of my friends back home who have given me up for lost. Thirty and not married. When I came out at eighteen I was supposed to find a husband. That's what it was about.
CASI	Would you like to try a sip of vodka?
CONSTANCE	(*Laughing*) Why?

11

CASI	Because in Russia when people settle back to talk about their lives they drink vodka or tea and there's no tea.
CONSTANCE	You're not Russian, you said.
CASI	No. But I live in what is called Russia. You said you're not English, but you talk about coming out. You look like an Englishwoman, you talk like an Englishwoman.
CONSTANCE	(*Angrily*) I'm not English, I'm Irish!
CASI	All right, all right! Where the devil is Janko? I'm starving.
CONSTANCE	I'll go out and get something for us.
CASI	You will not. I'd rather starve a bit longer and have you stay here. (*He massages her calf*) I enjoyed that trip, comrade Constance. (*Pause*) I expect at home you don't generally cycle. It wouldn't be considered proper.
CONSTANCE	I don't because I've always had such wonderful horses. You'd love my horses. And you'd love galloping on the shore and amongst the dunes.
	JANKO *enters*
JANKO	Sorry I was so long, but it's not as easy as you think this time of night. Here's your food and here's your wine and here's your change.
CASI	(*Looking at the money*) This isn't much!
JANKO	You just haven't kept pace with the cost of living.
CASI	You smell of wine.
JANKO	So what?
CASI	You take my money and my time to get drunk, that's what.
JANKO	Oh, look at old sobersides there! Never been known to have a drop too much brandy. I've had a few quick glasses. You don't call that drunk.
CONSTANCE	Thank you Janko. That's all right. You can go.
JANKO	Oh, can I?
CONSTANCE	(*Firmly*) Yes.
	JANKO *comes downstage to speak to audience.*
JANKO	Not many perks with this job. A bottle of Beaujolais from time to time – it has to be taken you understand

because he never gives it – a sip or two of vodka when he's not looking and that's about it. Perhaps she'll change his ideas a bit, what do you think? She's bound to have an effect on him. They're going to be inseparable. I don't need to tell you that, do I? Obvious isn't it? All set up for classic romance. What about the wife, did I hear you say? Ah, well ... CASMIR *sits head in hands.* CONSTANCE *kneels beside him. He is weeping distractedly.*

CONSTANCE Casi, don't. No more. Stop it now!

CASI (*Speaking through sobs*) What a waste, what a terrible waste! Both of them, Constance, both! I knew it had to come soon with her, but him too! A little child. Why?

CONSTANCE There's no reason. It just happens.

CASI It's my fault. She left everything to follow me. I abused her, betrayed her. Betrayed them all, my wife and my sons. It's God's punishment.

CONSTANCE If it were a punishment you would have been the one to die.

CASI The one who is left is the one who suffers. They are at peace.

CONSTANCE Casimir, you no longer had anything to do with your wife. It is not your fault.

CASI How can you say I no longer had anything to do with her?

CONSTANCE Did you? What sort of contact have you had over the past few years?

CASI A wife is a wife for ever. It is not something you can ignore. I had a wife even though I never saw her. I had two sons even though they would never recognise their father. Now I have only one.

CONSTANCE (*Puts her arms around him and cradles him*) You have one and you must take care of him. You must see him. You must have him to live with you.

CASI How can I?

CONSTANCE Of course you can.

JANKO (*To audience*) And that's how it was!

13

	CONSTANCE *and* CASIMIR *change positions. She sits. He kneels at her feet.*
CASI	If you say yes it will be until death. I'll never leave you alone anywhere. I'll never allow anyone near you with a disease. I'll take care of you, cherish you until I die.
CONSTANCE	I don't know.
CASI	Of course you don't know. How can you believe that I will look after you when I was so cold and cruel to my first wife?
CONSTANCE	I wouldn't ask for fidelity. I don't care about that. What does it matter if you enjoy other women?
CASI	I would go mad if you looked at another man. I mean, looked in a certain way.
CONSTANCE	(*Laughing*) I know.
CASI	Is that why you hesitate?
CONSTANCE	No. (*Pause*) I love you. I'm in love with you. You are my only love. It's something else.
CASI	I remember now. You're already married to Art. But you're not a Catholic. You could get a divorce.
CONSTANCE	I need time to think. Will you leave me alone for a few days? My sister Eva is coming to see me. I would like to spend time with her.
CASI	And talk things over?
CONSTANCE	Yes.
CASI	Does she approve of marriage?
CONSTANCE	I think so. (*Pause*) Do you love me?
CASI	I adore you. I would do anything for you. Ask me.
CONSTANCE	Just don't get in touch with me for four days.
	CASIMIR *rises and exits. Enter* EVA, *the sisters embrace.*
CONSTANCE	It's not much, but it's home for the moment.
EVA	Esther and I don't live in any luxury. It's nice, it suits you. You're looking well.
CONSTANCE	Which is more than I can say for you. You're very pale.
EVA	Manchester is not the best place in the world to put colour into your cheeks. Perhaps later in the year I

	can manage a fortnight in Lissadell. We're doing such good work, Constance. I wish you would come and see. Some of the women are wonderful. So brave and strong. So much to fight against, so little chance of winning. (*Pause*) But then it's so different from the life you're living here.
CONSTANCE	Is that a reproach?
EVA	No, oh no! (*She takes* CONSTANCE'S *hands*) Never, my dear. Whatever you do is what you must do. I want to share your life for four days, to learn what it feels like to be an art student in Paris. And to meet your friend Casimir.
CONSTANCE	You won't be allowed to do that yet. I want to show you Paris without him. It must be just you and me for a few days, Evie. (*Pause*) He's asked me to marry him.
EVA	(*Smiles*) Of course!
CONSTANCE	You're not shocked?
EVA	I expected it from everything you said. It could seem a bit soon, I suppose. Mother might think so. And then he is a Roman Catholic. With a son. And a foreigner. (*Teasing*) Just what we might have imagined for you, Constance!
CONSTANCE	You're assuming I'm going to accept.
EVA	Aren't you?
CONSTANCE	I'll tell you in in three days time. You'll put him into perspective. (*Pause*) We are already lovers.
EVA	(*Laughing*) Connie, why do you keep telling me things I already know?
CONSTANCE	How can you know that?
EVA	Your letters are full of him, you are clearly devoted to him. How could you not be lovers, alone here in this city? Who is to stop you?
CONSTANCE	What a woman of the world you sound. Especially – (*mischievously*) – for a spinster!
EVA	A spinster! I suppose that is what I am. I never think about it. I haven't time for marriage, Con, I really haven't.

15

CONSTANCE	I'm not sure that I have.
EVA	Of course you have and you've met this man and fallen in love.
CONSTANCE	I wasn't looking for a husband.
EVA	I know. We decided all that sort of silly nonsense wasn't for us a long time ago, didn't we?
CONSTANCE	Marriage was the only real thing for most of our friends.
EVA	They considered you and me beyond the pale, my love. I must admit, Con, I couldn't see you pairing off with anyone we knew. That's why I'm dying to meet your Casimir.
CONSTANCE	He's such fun.
EVA	I'm sure he is.
CONSTANCE	He's wildly handsome; there's a drawing I did of him. Look!
EVA	What beautiful eyes!
CONSTANCE	I may have made them a little larger than they are. They have such expression, though.
EVA	You've caught it well.
CONSTANCE	In a way, the best thing about him is his voice. His accent. No, the very best thing is his personality.
EVA	Why are you keeping him away from me for four days?
CONSTANCE	We won't mention him any more.
	JANKO *comes towards them.*
JANKO	Compliments of Count de Markievicz, Miss Gore-Booth. He has reserved a table for you and your sister tonight at Maxim's. The meal will be charged to his account. Tomorrow night there will be a box at your disposal at the Opera and the following night at the Opéra Comique. The Count himself leaves for the country tonight. A bicycle trip. He has asked me to look after you in his absence.
EVA	(*Claps her hands delightedly*) Marry him, Con, do marry him! (*To* JANKO) Will you dine with us?
JANKO	Oh no! I'll be waiting outside to get you a cab.
EVA	Why won't you eat with us? And come to the Opera

	and Theatre? Or do you have something else to do?
JANKO	Not a lot. There's always this and that, you know, a bit of polishing here, a bit of cleaning there.
CONSTANCE	Please join us Janko.
JANKO	I don't think that would be a good idea.
CONSTANCE	I'll take the responsibility.
JANKO	I think the table's reserved for two.
CONSTANCE	That's easily changed. It's a brilliant idea of Eva's. Casimir owes you a good meal or two.
JANKO	You're right there.
EVA	Wonderful. I'll feel much better about it all if you're with us.
JANKO	(*To* CONSTANCE) Promise you'll tell him the lady insisted. It's not my fault.
CONSTANCE	Promise.

JANKO *comes downstage. Speaks to the audience.*

JANKO   I won't say I didn't feel very uncomfortable to start with but after a couple of glasses of champagne I really started getting used to it. It's a good thing I was there because the champagne was waiting on the table and neither of these two drink much. Half a glass is about as much as they can take. It's a pity he's back Friday. No more high life for yours truly. I like Eva. No side to her. Even made me call Constance, Constance. She said it was silly dining with someone who called you Miss Eva and Miss Constance. I'll have to watch it now everything's back to normal. (*Thoughtfully*) Handsome woman. Considerate, gentle. In different circumstances . . .

Enter CASIMIR.

CASI	Janko!
JANKO	Sir!
CASI	Everything been all right?
JANKO	Fine. (*Pause*) No problem. They've asked you to dine with them this evening and to call round at six so that you and Ev . . . Miss Eva can get acquainted.
CASI	Do you think Constance is going to accept me?
JANKO	Oh yes, no doubt about it.

17

CASI	Janko! (*He throws his arm round him and kisses him on the mouth*) Go out and buy yourself some wine as a celebration. Here (*Gives him money*).
JANKO	Right! (*Looks at money, then at audience*) Enough for a very modest bottle of Beaujolais, I would say.
CASI	Before you go, get my evening clothes ready. And help me off with these boots. (*He sits*)
JANKO	(*Pulling off boots*) Been far, have we?
CASI	To Chartres.
JANKO	Ah!
CASI	I thought it was worth a pilgrimage, to say a few prayers for my future.
JANKO	Yes, your future. (*Pause*) I seem to remember a bit of your past lives in Chartres too.
CASI	(*Placing his finger on JANKO'S lips*) Not a word. JANKO *returns upstage.* CASIMIR *moves downstage to greet* EVA *and* CONSTANCE. *He clicks his heels in front of* EVA, *bows and kisses her hand.*
CASI	Miss Gore-Booth you are beautiful. I did not imagine any family could produce two such women. I thought Constance must be unique.
EVA	I am delighted to meet you, Casimir. I have so much enjoyed your hospitality. CASIMIR *kisses* CONSTANCE *on both cheeks.*
CASI	You have told your sister?
CONSTANCE	Yes. *Pause.*
CASI	(*Nervously*) If you could give me an answer now it would be most kind. I do understand that you might prefer to wait until later in private.
CONSTANCE	I tell Eva everything. Yes, Casi, yes. CASIMIR *gives a roar of delight and swings her off her feet. He looks across at* EVA.
CASI	May I kiss her in your presence?
EVA	Please do. CASIMIR *gives* CONSTANCE *a great kiss and hug.*
CASI	(*To* EVA) Now may I kiss *you*?

	EVA *opens her arms wide and* CASIMIR *hugs and kisses her.*
JANKO	(*To audience*) If it's a free for all, I wouldn't mind having a go!
CASI	Here is the ring. (*He gives her a ring*) We are now engaged.
EVA	(*Holding out her hands to them both*) I wish you every joy, my dears. Casimir, you're everything I could have wanted for Con. Whenever I thought of who she might marry, I had to invent an ideal suitor because the real ones were so unsatisfactory. I never invented anyone remotely like you, but I see you're just right.
	CASIMIR *kisses her hand.*
EVA	(*Turning to* CONSTANCE) Con, my love, I am so happy for you. (*She kisses her*) I don't know when I'll next see you. Perhaps in Ireland at Lissadell. Take good care of yourself.
	She moves away.
CONSTANCE	Wait. Casi, would you leave us for a while?
CASI	(*Pausing*) Of course. Au revoir, Eva. I look forward to getting to know you better.
EVA	Au revoir, Casimir.
	CASIMIR *moves away.*
CONSTANCE	You won't let things be changed between us now I'm engaged? I need to be close to you, Evie, I shall always need you to be close to me. Whatever happens.
EVA	You're going to be very busy.
CONSTANCE	I've always been busy. You're busier than I am, anyway.
EVA	Yes, I know. (*Pause*) But it *will* be different. *You* will be different. Just because you'll be a married woman with a home and a family. (*She laughs*) It will be a new Constance, Constance de Markievicz, not Constance Gore-Booth. We won't even have the same name any more, think of that! You'll be a Polish Countess. Will you paint under your new

	name? Will you even go on painting?
CONSTANCE	Of course I'll go on painting. I'm a painter. I've fought hard enough for that.
EVA	You and Casimir will be expected to do all the social rounds when you get back home. You won't be able to sneak away like you used to.
CONSTANCE	I will too, and he'll come with me. He won't want all that.
EVA	Won't he?
CONSTANCE	Of course he won't. You don't know him yet. You wait and see. Our life is going to be full of excitement. (*Pause*) I needed to meet him. I was beginning to feel restless. Casi has so much energy and more imagination than I have. Our lives will be splendidly creative!
EVA	(*Looks at her with affection*) I wish I had your energy, Con. I could do so much with it. (*She hugs her*) I wish you well. Goodbye.
CONSTANCE	Please take care of yourself. And write soon.
EVA	I will.
	EVA *comes downstage towards* JANKO, *holds out her hand.*
EVA	Goodbye, Janko, I'll be seeing you in Ireland.
JANKO	(*Takes her hand and shakes it*) I hope so Miss Eva.
EVA	(*Still holding his hand*) Thank you for looking after us.
JANKO	My pleasure.
	EVA *leaves the stage.* CASIMIR *strides grandly down towards* JANKO.
CASI	Janko, swords at dawn in the Bois de Boulogne, usual place.
JANKO	Yes sir.
	CONSTANCE *runs down, takes him by the arm.*
CONSTANCE	Casi, this is ridiculous. It was nothing! A silly remark. You know what flirts the French are.
CASI	They do not flirt with my fiancée. They do not touch her!
CONSTANCE	He didn't know I was your fiancée.
CASI	Too bad.

CONSTANCE	If it had been another woman would you have reacted in the same way?
CASI	Why should I?
CONSTANCE	If you thought him insulting?
CASI	One cannot leap to the defence of every woman's honour, only one's own woman.
CONSTANCE	What about defending myself?
CASI	How can you do that? Could you have knocked him down?
CONSTANCE	Perhaps. He didn't need to be knocked down. I don't need a man to look after me. You're my friend, not my bodyguard.
CASI	(*Takes her hand*) Constance, I have fought duels to protect my friends.
CONSTANCE	Only if you think they're too weak to fight for themselves. Otherwise they would feel dishonoured.
CASI	(*Releases her hand*) I don't want to talk about it any more.
	JANKO *moves upstage, tries to catch* CASIMIR'S *eye without being noticed by* CONSTANCE.
JANKO	(*Coughs*) Sir! (*Coughs again*) Sir, could I just have a word with you?
CASI	Is it important?
JANKO	Well yes, rather. Would you mind?
	CASIMIR *comes downstage towards* JANKO.
CASI	Well?
JANKO	Lady wants to see you urgently.
CASI	What lady?
JANKO	You know.
CASI	I don't know. Who?
JANKO	Jacqueline.
CASI	My ex-model?
JANKO	Exactly. Your *ex*-model. Not too happy about this 'ex' bit, it appears. Wants to see you, now, for an explanation. Won't go away.
CASI	But I wrote to her. Didn't you tell her . . . ?
JANKO	I told her. Wouldn't listen. A drop too much. I think you'd better see her, sir.

CASI	Damn! Damn, damn, damn!
	He moves off.
CONSTANCE	Janko!
JANKO	Madame!
CONSTANCE	Come here a minute will you?
	She moves slightly downstage. He crosses over to her.
CONSTANCE	What's wrong?
JANKO	Nothing. Just one of the Count's friends has a problem he needs advice about. Affair of the heart. He's in a bit of a state. Needs sorting out.
CONSTANCE	Is it a woman?
JANKO	A woman? Of course not.
CONSTANCE	It is. Is it his mistress?
JANKO	Ex-mistress, if you please ma'am.
CONSTANCE	Doesn't he see her any more?
JANKO	When does he have the time? I mean, of course he doesn't.
CONSTANCE	Does he miss her?
	Pause.
CONSTANCE	Does he miss her, Janko?
JANKO	No.
CONSTANCE	He does. Of course he does. I can't replace her. I'm not . . .
JANKO	Excuse me. I've just remembered something urgent.
CONSTANCE	Am I embarrassing you?
JANKO	Oh no. I just have to go.
CONSTANCE	You have to get used to me. You're going to live with me after all. We have to trust each other, you and I. CASIMIR *comes back towards them.*
CASI	I'm so sorry. It was a friend of mine in great distress. It's all right now.
CONSTANCE	Casi, are you sure you want to marry me? Just because we're engaged it doesn't mean you have to go through with it. I know you are attracted to fresh young women. I understand. I'm not like that. Why do you love me? I might not be enough for you. You must think of that. There is time.

22

CASI	(*Takes her in his arms*) I am absolutely certain I want to marry you. I am madly in love with you because you're bold, you're handsome and I want you to bear me a heroic son. (*He kisses her*)
JANKO	Signed, sealed and delivered you might as well say. We go to Ireland, meet the relations. Three weddings in London. Not bad, eh? One at a Registry Office, one at the Russian Legation, and the last at St Mary's, Marylebone! Not a Catholic church in sight. Her lot wouldn't have it. They cycled round Normandy for their honeymoon. Settled down here sort of. New studio in Paris. He's got lots of com- missions. Fourteen months after the wedding she had this baby, a girl. A studio in Montparnasse is not a proper environment to bring a baby up in, so she's left in Ireland with Grandma. He's now got two children, one in Russia and one in Ireland and he's as happy as a sandboy without either of them. She doesn't seem to worry overmuch either. They paint, they go out, they give parties. I'm asking him for a rise next week, the cost of living's going up some- thing terrible.
	CONSTANCE *comes forward with* CASIMIR.
CONSTANCE	Casi, I think I've persuaded your mother to let us have Stanislav with us. As long as he's not allowed to forget Polish and goes regularly to Mass.
CASI	You must have the charm of the devil. She's always been definite that Paris is no place for a child.
CONSTANCE	She still is. She's right. I'm getting tired of Paris myself. (*Pause*) My mother's found us a house in Dublin. It sounds wonderful. You'll love Dublin, we'll have so many friends. I know a lot of people, especially at the Castle. And the countryside and the sea will be right on our doorstep.
JANKO	So we arrive at St Mary's, Frankfurt Avenue with sixty-four cases of furniture and two bicycles, which are kept in the stables. Me and a maid. No gardeners, but a big garden. She's the one that likes getting her

hands in the soil. So she gets busy planting whilst he goes off to discover Irish whiskey with the Bohemian set. Dublin society centres round the Castle home of King Edward's Viceroy, Lord Dudley. The Count and Countess Markiewicz are what you might call an exotic addition to a more traditional circle. After all, they're still young – she's thirty-five and he's not thirty.

Dance music. CONSTANCE *and* CASIMIR *stand side by side but slightly turned away from each other, surveying the scene. He has a glass in his hand.*

CASI   You know Lady Dudley really is extraordinarily handsome! I would love to paint her. I couldn't do her justice, mind you, half her charm is in the way she moves.

CONSTANCE   She's been painted over and over again. I should think she's tired of sitting.

CASI   They say she's pregnant. It doesn't show, even in that dress. Perhaps I'll make a bid now to be the first to paint the mother and child. See the way she's standing? The line that goes right down through from the nape of the neck to the thigh. Superb.

CONSTANCE   Don't stare so, Casi.

CASI   (*Sips the drink*) How right you were to bring me here, my dear. I'm very comfortable in the city, with these people. They're wonderful, beautiful people. They have style.

CONSTANCE   There's Lady Sibell just arrived. I must have a word with her about the stall at the Irish Horticultural Society Spring Show. I thought we might do one together.

CASI   Good idea. We might see a bit more of her then.

CONSTANCE   (*Turns to look at him*) Casi!

CASI   Don't worry. I've told you before my love, I'll leave your friends alone. Lady Sibell would be nice to have around the house, that's all.

CONSTANCE   (*Turning away again*) Will you have a word with Lady Weldon later? She would like us to perform at

	one of her soirées. You singing your Polish songs, and me accompanying you.
CASI	That means we have to listen to half an hour of her whistling first. I don't know if I can bear it!
CONSTANCE	Don't be mean She's an excellent whistler. The Misses Arnott will be playing their violin and cello duet and Sir Anthony will be doing his recitations.
CASI	(*Groans*) Do we have to?
CONSTANCE	No. But it would be considered ungracious if we didn't. (*Pause, turns towards Casimir*) Casi, something happened on the way that I just can't get out of my mind. An image which keeps flashing in front of my eyes when I'm looking at the dancers. I'm sorry, I'm not myself tonight.
CASI	(*Takes her hand*) What is it? The coach didn't knock anyone down? That's happened to me. It was horrible. An old peasant fell under the horses, then the wheels went over him.
CONSTANCE	Oh no. Nothing that dreadful. It was ordinary, I suppose. It just affected me.
CASI	Tell me.
CONSTANCE	We were coming up to the gates, so all the carriages were slowing down. There was the usual row of beggars who crowded forward, stood on the running boards to thrust their hands out, you know how it is. This tiny little girl jumped up to go through her routine, but when she saw my furs and my diamonds, her eyes widened, her mouth fell open and she couldn't utter a word. She fell back into the road as we moved off. I turned round to see that she wasn't hurt – and this is what I keep seeing – her mother gave her such a slap that she went crashing into the wall. Those two faces, both of them pinched with hunger and cold, the mother's twisted with anger and disappointment, the daughter's pale with shock.
CASI	Those people behave like that all the time. They hit each other, they are violent. They are more natural than we are, that's all. It's their way.

25

CONSTANCE	You don't understand. All that I saw in that woman's look – the desperation, the humiliation. I can't explain.
CASI	Don't take it to heart my love. It's probably her own fault. Come and dance. *Dance music.* CASIMIR *bows, holds out his hand to* CONSTANCE, *who hesitates, then curtseys. They dance.*
JANKO	There we are, that's how life goes on. Miss Eva comes over from time to time. I still have a soft spot for her. *Enter* EVA.
EVA	I told Esther we'd meet her in half an hour.
CASI	Where are you going?
CONSTANCE	A meeting.
EVA	Esther and I had it arranged months ago. We shall get quite a good attendance. Constance said she'd like to come. (*She smiles*) I think it's for old time's sake as much as anything. She and I made quite stirring speeches in Sligo in our youth.
CASI	You're not speaking tonight?
CONSTANCE	I haven't planned to. *Pause.*
CASI	I thought you had grown out of politics. (*Pause*) I can understand it when you were girls, but generally a married woman has more immediate problems to worry about, doesn't she? I thought we were invited to supper with the Plunketts?
CONSTANCE	That's not until 8.30.
CASI	You'll have to change. We'll be late.
CONSTANCE	We will not be late.
CASI	You said the evening was important.
CONSTANCE	It is. This meeting won't interfere with it.
EVA	You think it's all a waste of time, don't you Casi?
CASI	Not for you. It's your choice to spend your life trying to persuade women to fight for something they don't need, and aren't likely to get. What's so important about the vote?

26

EVA	(*Calmly*) You know very well that amongst other things the vote is a symbol of equality.
CASI	I don't! I don't understand what you're talking about, I really don't. I'm not being difficult. Equality! What a word! Shades of the French Revolution. It's a political invention and I don't like politics. Enjoy yourselves. I'll see you later. I'm going to the Arts Club to talk about the things that are important to me. Poetry, painting, drama, music. I used to think they meant more to my wife than women's suffrage. Obviously I was wrong.
CONSTANCE	(*Puts her arms around him*) Don't be spiteful, Casi. (*She kisses him*) You know you're talking to a poet and a painter.
CASI	(*Rather pathetically*) I wanted you to look through my play before we went out to tell me whether you think it needs revision.
CONSTANCE	I promise to do it before I go to bed.
CASI	You'll be too tired.
CONSTANCE	I won't. Now say you're sorry to Eva for being so dismissive.
	CASIMIR, *with one arm round* CONSTANCE, *holds out his other arm towards* EVA. *She moves across towards him and puts her arm round his waist so that he is embracing them both in a big hug.*
CASI	Eva, I respect you *and* love you. (*Pause*) But some of those women are so dull, so serious. They can't laugh. Teach them to laugh and I might come to your next meeting.
EVA	Some of them have nothing to laugh about.
CASI	Everyone has something to laugh about. Life is ridiculous. You should hear the way the peasants laugh at home. Laughter, dancing, something more vital than discussion. (*He squeezes them, then lets go*) I'll be back before eight.
	EVA *crosses to* CONSTANCE, *takes her hands.*
EVA	You are still happy, Con?
CONSTANCE	Oh yes. (*Pause*) Why shouldn't I be?

27

EVA	No reason.
CONSTANCE	I have a delightful daughter, and a generous husband who has no malice in him. I have what most women long for. We are invited everywhere, sometimes it's as if we spend half our lives at the Castle.
EVA	I didn't need a speech to convince me. Just a simple yes or no!

EVA *and* CONSTANCE *look at each other for a long moment.*

CONSTANCE	No.
EVA	Is it Casi's infidelity?
CONSTANCE	No. He has quick little shameful affairs from time to time which he asks my forgiveness for. How could I blame him? Since Maeve's birth, I haven't wanted him in that way.
EVA	You're not in love with someone else?
CONSTANCE	No. (*Pause*) There's such a lack in me Eva. So much to do, so many friends and such emptiness! I am loved and I love, what else is there?
EVA	I don't know what to say. (*Pause*) We could do with more workers in Dublin if you wanted to get involved.
CONSTANCE	I've been doing a lot of thinking recently. Coming back from Paris to Dublin I've seen it differently. I have met people through the theatre and the Arts Club whose ideas are quite different from the Castle set. They've made me realise how ignorant I was about my own country. They've shown me what being Irish means.
EVA	What does it mean?
CONSTANCE	Anger, frustration, humiliation. Your language, your lands taken away, living with someone else's rules; foreign laws. Oh, it wasn't as if I didn't know that before. I did, but I didn't recognise it. In Lissadell, years ago, during one of those bad winters, when Mother and you and I would take food round the cottages, I went on my own to see Mother Sheyhan – you remember?

28

EVA	You mean the very old lady? She always seemed a hundred to me.
CONSTANCE	I don't think she was all that old. She was ill and worn down. That day, her grandson was visiting her. I'd never seen him before – he'd gone away with his parents to live. He watched me as I unpacked the basket. I was uncomfortable. I was 13 or 14. He was very handsome – about 20 or so. When the basket was empty, he took my hand, kissed it, bowed and said – 'Thank you, my dear Miss Gore-Booth, for giving us back one fraction of what you have taken from us. One day, I and my friends will come back and take the rest.'
EVA	I used to hate those trips out with Mother and her baskets; I always felt ashamed.
CONSTANCE	I didn't, until then. Even then I didn't know what he meant. Well, I do now. After rehearsals, we've come back here, and I've listened to the talking through the night. Casi just laughs and shrugs, but for me it is a revelation. There are some amongst them prepared to die rather than sign an oath of allegiance. And I understand; now, I understand.
EVA	All that is complicated, Con. And for those people we are the enemy.
CONSTANCE	I am certainly not the enemy. I shall show them that. I'm going to join their movement.
EVA	They'll never trust you. Look at yourself! Listen to yourself!
CONSTANCE	And I shall become a member of the political party, Sinn Fein. We ourselves, that means.
EVA	(*Smiling*) Yes, I do know that.
CONSTANCE	You knew more than I did. I was so ignorant.
EVA	Perhaps you should approach the women first. Many actresses and women in your new circle must belong to Maud Gonne's Daughters of Erin. They are totally devoted to the Irish cause. Isn't that what much of the new theatre is about?
CONSTANCE	(*Pause*) I don't think they like me. I'm a dilettante to them, a wealthy amateur who can't act very well but

29

	likes to show off on stage.
EVA	There you are! What did I tell you?
CONSTANCE	I'll start with the men. Then perhaps the women will accept me.
EVA	Whoever you start with, I think you'd better take off your finery and practise your Irish accent, Countess de Markiewicz!
CONSTANCE	(*Takes her arm*) Let's go to your meeting. We'll be late.
EVA	And don't forget to read Casi's script later. There's probably a part in it for you! *They move away.*
JANKO	It is autumn. A bitter east wind blows from the sea, spitting icy rain into the gutters of the back streets. There is a ball at the Castle as usual, with the coachmen queueing outside, dripping steadily on to the rumps of the miserable horses. Constance leaves early, radiant in her furs and her diamonds. She walks past the coaches and catches a tram. She gets out in one of the poorer suburbs, knocks on the door. CONSTANCE *comes downstage.*
CONSTANCE	(*Holds out her hand*) Good evening. I am Constance Markiewicz. You wrote to me after reading one of my speeches, suggesting I might like to join the Daughters of Erin and write for your new magazine. I would be very pleased to do so. I'm sorry about my clothes, I came straight from a ball. I won't appear like this again. *Blackout.*

PART II

An empty stage. The lights are up for several seconds, whilst the introduction to the Pirate King's song from the PIRATES OF PENZANCE *is played. At length* CASI *appears wearing a pirate's hat and jacket. He clears his throat and begins to sing.*

CASI   Better far to live and die
Under the great black flag I fly
Than play a sanctimonious part
With a pirate head and pirate heart.
Enter CONSTANCE. *She is very simply dressed by comparison with the first part. She is holding a sheaf of notes. She looks at the audience when she speaks.*

CONSTANCE   A few jottings from my contribution to the Daughters of Erin's new magazine. Gardening notes. In order that our native flowers and trees may grow freely, we must be severe in dealing with the pests which eat at their roots and sap their lifeblood. We must be ruthless in hacking back the alien weeds, we must wage constant war on slugs and snails. A good nationalist can only regret that she cannot crush the nation's enemies as she can the garden's, with one tread of her fairy foot.

CASI   Among the cheating world go you
Where pirates all are well-to-do
But I'll be true to the song I sing
And live and die a Pirate King.

CONSTANCE   Ireland, like the garden, lies sleeping and resting, recouping her vital powers for the struggle that will come. (*She shuffles her notes*) Exhortations to the young. A 'Moral Force' movement, a movement that

31

stops short of shedding blood; and therefore forbids
you to make the last sacrifice – that of your life –
cannot be taken seriously and therefore must end in
contempt and ridicule. Learn to discipline and be
disciplined, learn to shoot, learn to scout, learn to
give up all for Ireland.

She leaves her notes and looks directly at audience.
During CASI'S *next verse she turns towards him to*
watch his performance. Aware of this, he plays up to it.

CASI When I sally forth to seek my prey
I help myself in a Royal way.
I sink a few more ships it's true
Than a well-bred monarch ought to do.
But many a King on a first-class throne
If he wants to call his crown his own,
Must manage somehow to get through
More dirty work than ever I do.

CONSTANCE *joins in the chorus, crosses over to*
him and they both do a little dance. When they've
finished, she hugs him.

CONSTANCE Bravo, Casi, you'll be perfect. I'll be so proud of
you.

CASI I thought we should give a big party at the end of the
run. Everyone must dress as a character from a
Gilbert and Sullivan opera. We'll have an orchestra.

CONSTANCE What a marvellous idea! I'll organise it before I go.

CASI Go?

CONSTANCE Oh Casi, you've forgotten Manchester!

CASI What do you mean? I've never been there! How can
I remember it?

CONSTANCE You haven't forgotten that I'm going there a fort-
night today?
Pause.

CASI (*Sombrely*) How can you forget what you didn't
know?

CONSTANCE I told you, you just weren't listening.

CASI How long will you be gone?

CONSTANCE Three weeks.

CASI	But that will bring us right up to the time of beginning rehearsals for my new play.
CONSTANCE	I'm taking the script with me. I'll learn my part in bed.
CASI	Why do you have to go?
CONSTANCE	I don't *have* to. Though they do need everyone they can get to help. It's important they win this by-election. I *want* to go. The experience of fighting a campaign might be very useful.
CASI	What for?
CONSTANCE	The future. Now, how many people are you wanting to come to this party? And how many courses do you think they'll be needing to eat?

Enter JANKO. *Speaks to audience.*

JANKO	Amongst his friends he's known as very easy-going. They all have a good laugh at her. After all, it's not really serious, when you're part of the inner circle of highest Dublin Society, to try to make an alliance with the other side. It's a kind of affectation to be seen with the Viceroy at the Opera but to refuse to stand for the national anthem. And to talk about the poor whilst you're counting out the asparagus tips for a dinner party for twenty! But he just takes it in his stride. So far. He's not too keen on Manchester, though!

CASI *stands back as* EVA *and* CONSTANCE *take centre stage.*

CONSTANCE	But you must have a rest after this campaign. You look so tired. You mustn't get ill. You can't afford to become ill.
EVA	You know I'm never ill. I'm like you. We had a hard training when we were young. I'm grateful for that. When I'm asked what I know of hardship – 'What can Miss Gore-Booth tell us about deprivation? I believe Miss Gore-Booth was a debutante?' At least I can tell them that I was often cold and frequently hungry because I'd been sent to bed with no supper, that I learnt to be as tough as the boys.
CONSTANCE	It's not the same.

EVA	(*Pause*) No, I know. It's something, but not much.
CONSTANCE	It's nothing. Everything at Lissadell was a privilege. Going hungry was a privilege, because it taught us what it could feel like, every once in a while. Being cold was a privilege because we learnt to withstand it. And there was always a fire if you looked for it. We had the sea and the sky, the clean bright air. I felt sick in those little back streets, Eva. Sick for the poor little pale people forced to live and die there. They are starving and choking to death.
EVA	I got over that sickness after the first year here. And the shame about what I'd had. I realised the only right way to live was to use the strength I'd been given to fight for those who had none.
CONSTANCE	I'm enjoying it, though, Evie. I'm enjoying speaking to the crowds, arguing, persuading. I'm myself. I've written to Casi telling him I must stay for the count. We'll have to put off rehearsals for a couple of days. Or he can start without me. It's not important.
	EVA *exits.* CASI *comes forward.*
CASI	Act I, scene V, Constance. I need to go over that with you on your own.
CONSTANCE	(*Moving towards him*) I think we should talk about it first.
CASI	We don't need to talk about it, I wrote it, I'm direct-ing it, you do what I tell you.
CONSTANCE	I have to believe in what I am doing.
CASI	Are you telling me this play is unbelievable?
CONSTANCE	Of course not, darling. It's just that I have to find my own way of understanding the character. The way you're asking me to do it is uncomfortable.
CASI	Uncomfortable!
CONSTANCE	Lady Alathea is a very passionate woman. This scene, where she has to tell her husband she is in love with someone else . . .
CASI	Yes?
CONSTANCE	Could I just show you what I would do and say if it were me?

CASI	It is not you. (*Rather bitterly*) It could never be you to lose your head over a man.
CONSTANCE	I know it's not me. But an actress has to imagine herself into situations she would never be in, doesn't she?
CASI	She does what her director tells her, it's simple. I know better than you. I know women like that. Lots of them. Some of them have fallen for me like she falls for Archie Longhurst.
CONSTANCE	I find it a little difficult because I don't like Archie Longhurst.
CASI	Why?
CONSTANCE	He's cold, unpleasant, doesn't believe in anything but himself. How can you fall in love with that?
CASI	Constance . . .
CONSTANCE	I'm not criticising the play, my love. It's my lack of understanding that's to blame.
CASI	Quite! He is not a nice man. He is a dilettante, that is the point.
CONSTANCE	I know it is the point.
CASI	You don't like him, that's fine. The audience is not supposed to like him.
CONSTANCE	But Lady Alathea is supposed to love him!
CASI	Well imagine it as . . . mainly physical!
	They look at each other and burst out laughing.
CASI	All right, forget that one.
CONSTANCE	I'll make a big effort, I really will. Please just let me do this scene my way. Without the lines. I don't quite know them yet.
CASI	You said . . .
CONSTANCE	I meant to. There was absolutely no time. We were up until two and three o'clock every morning and awake again at six. So much to do, so much to organise I never imagined!
CASI	No wonder Eva is so thin. I don't like women to be so thin. They're not women any more. She and Miss Roper have forgotten how to be women. Don't ever do that, Con.

35

CONSTANCE	I'll have the lines exactly tomorrow.
JANKO	(*To audience*) You've got to expect a bit of temperament, haven't you? It isn't her kind of play. Mind you, she has her effect on him. He writes his nationalist piece with the best of them. 'The Memory of the Dead'. Goes down a bomb, as you might say, with the critics.
	CONSTANCE *marches downstage as if carrying a rifle.*
CONSTANCE	Left, left, left right, left. About turn! Left, left, left right left. Halt. Attention! (*Pause*) Shoulder arms! Take aim. Fire! Lower arms. Stand easy.
JANKO	Good grief!
CONSTANCE	Most of you boys have never seen a gun before, I know. Pass this one round amongst you. (*She holds out the gun.* JANKO *takes it*) At the moment you have no use for it. But you might. It is essential that you know how to use it, that you feel at home with it, for it could become your most influential friend. We shall do drill every time we meet because that way you will feel familiar, and you will learn discipline. My boys will learn to be quick and confident and controlled. We'll break for tea now, then we'll reassemble on the lawn for signalling practice.
	CASI *strolls over to* JANKO. *He is holding a glass in his hand.*
CASI	Janko.
JANKO	Sir?
CASI	Who are those boys out there on the lawn? What kind of game is Constance playing with them?
JANKO	They are her Red Hand Knights, sir. Started them up whilst you were away. Nationalist Youth Movement.
CASI	But there are only eight of them! They look very weak and bewildered. Some of them can't stand up properly. By the way, I will not have you drinking my whiskey! Do you take me for a fool? I know how much I left.
JANKO	Me take you for a fool sir? Never. I never touched

	your booze, but I did see the lads wandering round the sitting room earlier on.
CASI	You think those sprouts drank my whiskey?
JANKO	Just look at them. What do you think?
CASI	I think I locked the cupboard. You know where the key is, they don't.
JANKO	Could be that getting into locked cupboards is one of the skills the Countess is teaching them.
CASI	Are they going to be around often?
JANKO	I reckon so. She's taking them to camp next week.
CASI	Here, go out and buy half a dozen bottles of whiskey. And don't be long.

CONSTANCE *moves across to* CASIMIR.

CONSTANCE	Casi, you know my mother's engaged an English governess for Maeve?
CASI	Has she?
CONSTANCE	An English governess!
CASI	(*Shrugs*) They are supposed to be the best. (*Pause*) And your Mother is from an English military family.
CONSTANCE	If she thinks she's going to have an influence on my daughter, she's crazy. Maeve is to be brought up learning Irish history and Irish beliefs and attitudes.
CASI	(*Gently*) It is very difficult to control your daughter's education when you live so far away. We see Maeve three or four times a year for a few days.
CONSTANCE	We must go down there next week – for a month.
CASI	We are beginning rehearsals of my new play in three weeks' time.
CONSTANCE	You stay as long as you can. I'll stay for a month. We shall visit historic monuments, go on picnics. We shall place stones on Queen Maeve's cairn.
CASI	(*Laughing*) And then when we've left, her grandmother will tell her tales of Yorkshire and cut out pictures for a scrapbook of the Royal Family.
CONSTANCE	I will not have that innocent child's mind filled with ideas which have no place in her future.
CASI	You cannot prevent it. (*Pause*) What is your daughter to you, Con? When we visit, you are all delight. It is

37

never-ending kisses and hugs. Scampering of children and dogs and games in the orchard. When we leave, it is tears and more hugs and clingings-on as if separation were the hardest thing in the world to bear. Here there is no room, no time for that. Here it is all speeches and articles and pack-drill with the boys and parties for sympathisers with the cause. Here Maeve doesn't exist.

CONSTANCE She exists every moment. I love her Casi, I love her so much it is painful. But it's wrong for her to be here when she has her grandmother's love to wrap around her every moment. I adore her, yet I cannot give her all the love I feel. My time must be given to others, to my boys, to the Daughters of Erin.

CASI No time for Maeve. No time for Stanislav.

CONSTANCE Stanislav is at a good school.

CASI He's out of your way. (*Pause*) Is he better off than with his grandparents? He is Russian Polish. What is he doing in this country? Why have we torn him from everything he knows just to throw him in a 'good school'?

CONSTANCE I love him, you love him. The school terms are not long. When he comes home he is with his father, where he should be. He loves me too, Casi.

CASI Of course he loves you. Everybody loves you. Maeve loves you, Stanislav loves you, I love you, the servants at Lissadell love you, the Dublin poor love you, but that's not the point. What's the good of loving someone who's always going out or going away? (*Pause*) Many people think you're a bad mother and a bad wife.

CONSTANCE Do you? Do you think that?

CASI Not in your heart. Your heart is full of love for us, we know that. But we don't have from you what most husbands and children take for granted. We don't come first in your life. (*Wistfully*) I did once. (*Pause*) Did you grow ashamed of me, amongst your new friends? My dissolute life? My drinking? My lack of

38

	seriousness? Have they turned you against me?
CONSTANCE	(*Puts her arms around him*) No, Casi, no. I can't blame you.
CASI	These are not my people. I can't pretend.
CONSTANCE	I know.
CASI	I've tried to talk their language. Even at the Arts Club where they like me, accept me, I'm a foreigner. I came here to be with you.
	Pause.
CONSTANCE	Let's go to the cottage. Now. Let's leave now. Spend the night there, two nights. Just you and me.
CASI	Your meetings . . .
CONSTANCE	The others will take care of them. I'm not indispens-able.
CASI	I had other plans.
CONSTANCE	(*Lets go of him*) Oh. I'm sorry. How thoughtless of me.
CASI	You don't know what I do when you're not here. I have to look out for myself, Con. I was to visit a lady in Francis Street, whom I drop in on from time to time. You know my needs.
	Pause.
CASI	Shall I cancel Francis Street?
CONSTANCE	Do you want to? Do you still want to spend a night in the country alone with me?
CASI	Janko!
JANKO	At your service!
CASI	Please tell Mrs Maloney I won't be able to see her tonight. Unexpected circumstances. I'll be in touch. Take her . . . a bunch of roses.
JANKO	Red?
CASI	No. Pink or white. Not red.
JANKO	(*To audience*) She'll throw herself wholeheartedly into his next production. And they're going on tour with it to Belfast. About time she paid him more attention, I say. I may complain about him some-times, but basically I'm on his side.
	CONSTANCE *and* CASIMIR *move slightly down-*

	stage arm-in-arm.
CASI	Thank God, we'll never have to worry about that damned donkey again. It's the last time I'm using an animal in a play. It was a nice idea, but I didn't understand donkeys. How could I? Horses are much more intelligent. You did so well as Eleanor, my dear. I was so proud of you. (*Pause*) Constance I'm proud of you!
CONSTANCE	(*Absently*) Thank you dear, I'm proud of you too.
CASI	I thought for my next production of the Devil's Disciple I might use your boys as part of the crowd. We need fifty extras so I thought we could have Trinity students and Nationalists and your boys. Would they do it?
CONSTANCE	What?
CASI	Would your boys appear as part of a crowd?
CONSTANCE	What would they have to do?
CASI	Fight the soldiers.
CONSTANCE	They'd love it. Yes.
	Pause.
CASI	What are you thinking about?
CONSTANCE	About all the people we've met, the things we've done. About James Connolly.
CASI	Ah!
CONSTANCE	Don't you find him inspiring?
CASI	He's a good talker.
CONSTANCE	I'm so glad we took the play to Belfast and we actually met the Connollys properly.
CASI	I seem to remember you were equally infatuated with that other demagogue in Dublin, Jim Larkin. 'A great primeval force' you called him.
CONSTANCE	Don't exaggerate!
CASI	Those were your exact words. So you have a new hero now. I'm surprised. Mr Connolly is not nearly as handsome.
CONSTANCE	(*Breaks away from him*) Casi, don't try to belittle them. They are fearless and inspired.
CASI	Whilst I play around with amateur theatricals?

CONSTANCE	You? Why bring yourself into it? There's no comparison.
CASI	I realise that. (*He bows*) I'm sorry, Countess, to have proved so inadequate.
CONSTANCE	(*Angrily*) Don't be silly.
CASI	No, *I'm* not being silly. *You* are. Talk to me properly. About you and me.
CONSTANCE	I want to talk to you about the organisation of labour.
CASI	I'm not interested in the organisation of labour.
CONSTANCE	You must be. We must all be. It is vital for our future.
CASI	All right. I'll talk about the organisation of labour and our future. What are we going to do, you and me? How are we going to organise our labours? Are you going to work with me in the theatre, are we going to paint sometimes, or are you going to follow your new pied piper?
CONSTANCE	Why are you turning the important into the trivial?
CASI	To me it is important, profoundly important. Nothing matters more than our relationship.
CONSTANCE	Our relationship isn't being called into question.
CASI	I am calling into question. Is it me or James Connolly?
CONSTANCE	That is ridiculous! It's like asking whether it is you or Ireland.
CASI	Connolly isn't a country nor an abstraction. He's a man. Are you in love with him?
CONSTANCE	Oh Casi, Casi! Think of him – short, bowlegged, thick neck, stolid. I am in love with his ideas. *Pause.*
CASI	Perhaps that is worse.
CONSTANCE	(*Takes his arm again*) I'll speak to the boys tomorrow and get them along to a rehearsal as soon as you like. And then we'll have a great party at the end of it all for everybody. The best party we've ever given!
JANKO	(*To audience*) It is also a birthday party for one of their friends, who is supplying the whiskey. The Count is supplying the champagne. Countess Con

	provides the beer and the food and the usual gallons of tea. She's made the biggest cake you've ever seen.
CASI	A last glass of champagne, Con, before we go to bed.
CONSTANCE	But it's five o'clock already.
CASI	What does time matter? What is five o'clock?
CONSTANCE	(*Slowly*) It's when working people get up to go to their factories.
CASI	None of that tonight. Here! Drink to the next successful production. To you and me and the theatre. My anchor in Dublin.
CONSTANCE	Here's to your anchor in Dublin! (*Drains a glass*) I don't really like champagne.
CASI	Just drink it! You look beautiful tonight. You grow more beautiful. I like you when you dress up as you dressed when we first met.
CONSTANCE	Don't get nostalgic. We've not been married long enough for that.
CASI	It is at least two lifetimes ago.
CONSTANCE	What do you mean?
CASI	You have changed. Like a caterpillar. You were a caterpillar when I met you, then you became a chrysalis and now you emerge as a moth.
CONSTANCE	I'd prefer a butterfly!
CASI	No. A moth. They rush to the light and the flames and destroy themselves.
CONSTANCE	How could you have fallen in love with a caterpillar?
CASI	You are the gardener! You should know some moth caterpillars are very handsome. And you can keep them in a box and give them the right things to eat and they are content, they don't fly away. (*Pause*) Thank you for tonight. (*He takes her glass, puts it down with his, takes both her hands and gazes soulfully at her*) Thank you, thank you.
CONSTANCE	(*Embarrassed, draws her hands away*) It was a good party. A strange mixture, but a good party.
CASI	It worked. The play worked. I shall do it again. I shall put on Strife and use real labourers. I shall pay them 1/6d a night. You'll like that won't you?

CONSTANCE	Yes, I will.
CASI	My theatre will mean something. More than my portraits. It will mean something, won't it Con? *Pause.*
CONSTANCE	Of course.
CASI	(*Flaring up suddenly*) Of course, she says, when she means 'of course not'. You give parties for the actors, you are there on first nights, you even play leading roles, but you think it is all without significance.
CONSTANCE	(*Wearily*) I'm not going to argue. It's too late.
CASI	It has been to late for a long time.
CONSTANCE	I'm going to bed.
CASI	Because you have to get up to organise your training camp.
CONSTANCE	Yes.
CASI	I hope you can get into your bed. There's probably someone asleep in it already. And in mine. After all, we keep open house, don't we? Leave the windows open so those in need can climb in and take shelter for the night. It's always interesting to see who's late for breakfast. There's always tea and bread and butter for sick boys, or sacked factory girls, always a place for anyone who can stand the noise of your printing press pounding away endlessly. There's always talk and laughter and drilling and planning, never a moment of peace and quiet and solitude.
CONSTANCE	Goodnight, Casi.
CASI	No! No! (*He moves to block her path*) You are not going away. (*He grabs her arms*) Why don't you answer me?
CONSTANCE	You haven't asked me a question. (*Pause*) I have nothing to say. It's all true.
CASI	And that's the way it will always be from now on?
CONSTANCE	Yes.
CASI	And you think you can make up for that with the occasional gesture towards my friends, my interests?
CONSTANCE	I'm not making up for anything. There's nothing to

	make up for. (*Pause*) Why are you saying all this now? We had such a good time.
CASI	That is why. We have fewer and fewer good times. Even tonight I could tell you thought it all a waste of time. You were a good hostess, you did your best and I'm grateful, I mean it, but your heart wasn't in it.
CONSTANCE	It's hard to put your heart into a party when you know so much about the struggle for existence a few streets away.
CASI	But you agreed to give it. It was your idea.
CONSTANCE	I know. I wanted to. For your sake, and for all your friends.
CASI	Who were once *our* friends.
CONSTANCE	(*Takes his hands*) I'm sorry if I was distracted. I can't help it. We are moving into exciting times. There will be action, confrontation. And we must be ready. We shall be ready, you'll see. We shall use every means, we shall use theatre to call people together, to give them courage for the battle.
CASI	(*Takes his hands away*) Don't include me in this 'we' you talk of.
CONSTANCE	But I do. You are with us, you know you are. *Pause.*
CASI	You are right, you need to sleep at least a little. Goodnight Constance. *They move apart and away.*
JANKO	(*To audience*) They tell me things are changing. It would seem that most of the working men of the city have been getting together. Don't want to put up with the way things are any more. Everybody's joining a union. It's the only way to fight for their rights, they say. We have just come back from the Ukraine. Me and him and Stanislav. We had a good time. First time I'd been home for years. He changed over there. More like his old self, know what I mean. We've come back for the Horse Show. Big event in Dublin, of course. A bunch of his mates met us at the station. So he's brought them home for a bit of a party.

CASI	(*Calling*) Constance! Constance! Where the devil is she? Constance! Janko go and have a look for her. I can't find any food except this damned bread and butter. There must be something else. I must feed my friends. We must have something in for the Horse Show Week, we'll be having visitors all the time – they need to eat!
JANKO	I think she's upstairs with a whole group of people, sir. There seems to have been a lot of excitement and there's talk of police and detectives and I couldn't quite follow what had been happening.
CASI	For heaven's sake! Go and give everyone downstairs some whiskey – I expect the upstairs lot are drinking tea – and then ask Constance to come down and explain what is going on. If she's too busy to do that then ask her just to tell me if there's anything any-where in this house to offer hungry guests apart from brown bread.
JANKO	Right. (*Moves upstage*)
	CONSTANCE *moves downstage towards* CASI, *takes hold of his hands.*
CONSTANCE	Welcome home, love. Did you enjoy it? I hope your sister-in-law's recovered from her 'flu. Where's Stanislav?
CASI	He went straight to bed. He was exhausted. He would have said hello, but he couldn't find you.
CONSTANCE	I know. I'm sorry. A lot has been happening. I've been rushing about all over the place.
CASI	Have we anything to eat?
CONSTANCE	There's plenty of bread. (*Sees the look on his face*) No. There's been no time to think about that.
CASI	I see. Well my party is more aware of the ordinary pleasures of life than your party.
CONSTANCE	Don't be irritable.
CASI	Look, I'm tired and hungry and I've had a terrible journey.
CONSTANCE	I'll send out for something. I'm sorry. I'm sure there are some eggs somewhere. I'll make you an omelette.

45

CASI	And my friends?
CONSTANCE	They'll have to fend for themselves.
CASI	Find me the eggs. I'll make my own omelette. You obviously have more important things to do.
	Pause.
CONSTANCE	Casi, listen. So much has happened while you were away. Tonight it all came to a head. Please, please bear with me. The working men and women of this city are fighting for their dignity, their future, their self-respect as human beings. We're in the middle of a strike. The tramworkers are locked out. Jim Larkin has been arrested and let out on bail.
CASI	Jim Larkin again! If it's not James Connolly, it's Jim Larkin. You are completely obsessed with these power maniacs.
CONSTANCE	Just let me tell you what happened today. Larkin was freed yesterday and today he made a public speech which would have roused you like it roused me – like it roused the hundreds listening. He took a piece of paper from his breast pocket and held it high in the air 'With your permission' he said, 'I am going to burn the Proclamation of the King'. Then he took a match, struck it, lit the corner of the paper – 'People can make Kings,' he said, 'and people can unmake them . . . I am a rebel and the son of a rebel. I recognise no law but the people's law.'
CASI	Words, words, words. The Irish have always been good at words.
CONSTANCE	The police immediately issued a second warrant for his arrest.
CASI	Of course. You provoke. They react. What do you expect?
CONSTANCE	There's a big meeting planned for tomorrow in O'Connell Street. He must be there. So he's gone into hiding.
CASI	Why are you telling me about these games? I am not interested. They have nothing whatever to do with me, the tramworkers, and the dockworkers and the

mill workers of Manchester. Nothing, nothing! And if you weren't so bedazzled by your Larkins and your Connollys you'd realise they have nothing to do with you. Leave that to Eva, go back to painting. Play in your garden, play with the Daughters of Erin, if you like, they're harmless, they're just like you, wealthy women with consciences. Play with your boy scouts if you must. At least that's healthy, but leave the workers to look after themselves. You don't understand them.

CONSTANCE   I can't.

CASI   You can. You're not involved, you're a camp follower, wanting to be where the excitement is, running round after the soldiers.

CONSTANCE   I can't. Larkin's here. Upstairs.
Pause.

CONSTANCE   (*Her voice trembling slightly*) I'm not on the side-lines. I'm in the thick of it.

CASI   (*Very violently*) How dare you hide that man in my house! How dare you expose me and my son to the consequences of your senseless passion for national-ist politics! Bear with you! I have borne with you ever since I agreed to follow you here. I've seen you gradually dragged deeper and deeper into the clutches of these fanatics. I've watched you change from a loving tolerant woman to a bigot who can hate people she doesn't even know, who was born in England, who has half her family living in England, but who speaks of the English as though they were no longer human beings. And I've borne with you, because I love you. I still love you in spite of what you've become. I thought you were still my wife, still cared for me as well as Ireland; had some con-sideration for my feelings. Was I wrong? Was I? What am I to you any more? What are we to each other? Do we give each other anything at all?
They stare at each other. Long pause. He holds out his arms. She goes to him, they hug each other and remain enfolded.

CONSTANCE	Will you lend him some of your clothes?
CASI	(*Hugging her tight*) Is it absolutely necessary?
CONSTANCE	He must be disguised when we take him into the Imperial Hotel, otherwise the authorities will have him before he can utter a word.
CASI	This isn't theatre, Con. It's for real. They might arrest you.
CONSTANCE	I'm ready for that.
CASI	(*Kissing her hair*) I'm not. If a policeman lays a finger on you, I'll . . . I'll challenge him to a duel.
CONSTANCE	Will you come with us tomorrow then?
CASI	I'll come with you, with my wife. To make sure you get away safely.
CONSTANCE	If you once heard him speaking to that crowd, you'd be converted. They're all with him. The force of the love must gather you in too.
CASI	I'll make sure you get away safely.
JANKO	(*To audience*) And he does, just. Touch and go. Listen, I'll tell you how it was. The crowds went mad when Jim Larkin stepped on to the balcony and began to speak. Pretty stupid, the Dublin police. They were lining the road three deep just outside the hotel, convinced Larkin would be appearing when all good Catholics come out from Mass. The hungry strikers had watched him walk calmly through the front entrance in a frock coat and top hat. A deaf old gentleman with a niece to interpret for him. He had to pretend to be deaf so as he wouldn't have to speak until he went out there in front of the masses. You see his voice would have given him away. This champion of Irish rights has a Liverpool accent! Right through the foyer he walked, right through the midst of his enemies and up the stairs. Into the dining room, past the waiters giving a last shine to the crystal and silver. Threw wide open the French windows and stepped on to the balcony. Even the law recognised him this time. Before he has a chance to deliver more than a sentence or two they rush in

and place him under arrest. The crowd sees the Countess, who is by now, as you might imagine, a well-known figure, and asks her to make a speech. She just leaps up out of her car and yells, 'Three cheers for Larkin'. Now that really does put the cat among the pigeons. Without more ado the peelers charge, swiping anyone they could reach with their batons. One of them had his arm raised to crack the Countess's skull when old Casimir digs his pipe in his back and says, 'Another step and you're a dead man'. The terrified peeler freezes on the spot and Casimir drags Constance back to the car and holds her down until they can drive away. And then the battle really rages. Bottles, bricks, stones, anything. At the end of the day, nobody had won. Now perhaps we'll be able to get on with the Horse Show.

CASI *brings* CONSTANCE *centre stage, sits her down, kneels in front of her, takes her hands, looks anxiously into her face.*

CASI   You're sure you're not bruised?

CONSTANCE   I may be bruised, but nothing's broken, that's certain, which is more than a good many will be able to say at the end of today. (*She tries to get up*) I must go back to Liberty Hall, that's where they'll be taking the wounded.

CASI   (*Pushes her down*) No, Constance! I forbid it! (*Sees her quizzical look*) I just won't let you. I'll carry you upstairs and lock you up.

CONSTANCE   They'll need bandages and iodine and then soup.

CASI   They'll have them!

CONSTANCE   They won't.

CASI   How many more times do I have to tell you this is madness! You're crazy, out of your mind! They have their own people, their own organisers from their own kind, without Lady Bountiful with her soup ladle hovering around, getting in their way. It is a workers' confrontation, workers, labourers, desperate men and women. How can you ever hope to become of them? You're an outsider.

CONSTANCE   Then why was it me they called on to make a speech
when Jim Larkin was arrested?
Pause.

CASI   I don't know.

CONSTANCE   Jim and I have stood side by side this last month, we
spoke together at almost every public meeting. I am a
leader in the Labour Movement, and the fight is only
beginning. Organisation is essential to keep up morale.
James Connolly will be coming down from Belfast to
help. He'll be staying here. It's the best place.

CASI   Oh yes, it's the best place. Very convenient, the
Countess's house. I can see why you're useful to
them. A big house, money to spend, not a lot it's true,
but some. And best of all their prize convert. Indeed
your accent, your aristocratic airs may be all to the
good. We have authority, you and I, we were born to
it. They can use that, they can use you – your accent,
your love, your energy, even your beauty. You're not
a person to them, you're a symbol.

CONSTANCE   I don't care – all they can use I want to give. I don't
care, Casi. I believe what they, we, are trying to do is
the only thing worth doing. I believe it with all my
heart and soul as I've never believed anything
before.
*Pause. CASI gets up, moves away. CONSTANCE
stands.*

CONSTANCE   You could come and cut bandages whilst I dress the
wounds.
CASI is silent, turned away from her.

CONSTANCE   I thought last night you'd understood.
Pause.

CASI   (*Turning towards her*) Constance for God's sake
break with them now before it's too late. Stay here
with me, I beg of you.

CONSTANCE   I'm sorry, I've gone too far . . . there's no turning
back. (*Pause*) I think I'd rather die than have the
shame of betraying my comrades.

50

	Long pause. They look at each other.
CASI	Perhaps you'll bring me home a bowl of soup. Au revoir, madame. Bonne soirée. Amusez-vous bien! CONSTANCE *opens her mouth to reply, closes it and moves away.* CASI *looks at her back with complete desolation, then begins to sob. They reach an agonising crescendo, then stop.*
CASI	(*Furiously*) Janko!
JANKO	(*Extremely nervous*) Sir!
CASI	Get me a bottle of vodka.
JANKO	I don't know if I can. There's plenty of whiskey.
CASI	God damn this country! Get me a bottle of whiskey then. Bring two glasses. We'll drink together and talk about Poland.
JANKO	Oh! Well, I did have an arrangement. It's usually my night off, if you remember.
CASI	Cancel it! Take tomorrow night off instead. Take the week off. I don't care. What does it matter? Go off with your friend to look at horses. Tonight I need you.
JANKO	Yes sir, but sir . . .
CASI	Don't argue with me! You are to bring me a bottle of whiskey, no, two bottles, and two glasses and tell me all about your parents and your grandparents and your brothers and sisters, especially your sisters. Your sister, Anna, I want to know more about her.
JANKO	She's engaged.
CASI	You surprise me! The night before we left Zywotowka – never mind. What are you waiting for? Do as I tell you!
JANKO	At once. (*He turns, comes downstage. Speaks to audience*) Bang goes my little bit of fun for the week. I don't think she'll take it too well. *He crosses upstage, fetches two bottles and two glasses. He opens one, pours a glass for* CASI, *offers it to him.* CASI *indicates that he should pour more into the glass, which he does. He then pours one for himself.*

51

CASI	I don't much care for Ireland. I don't even like Dublin any more. I like my friends, I love my friends, that's all. I would fight any man for Martin Murphy just as I would defend Dubronsky. I don't care that one is Irish and one is a Pole. I drink with them, I laugh with them, we enjoy life together. They are not my comrades. I hate that word. Comradeship used to mean a deep bond between two human beings. Now it means something else. It makes me shiver. It is so political. (*Raises his glass*) Let us drink to all our true friends.
JANKO	To all our true friends.
	CASI *drains the glass, holds it out for more.* JANKO *fills it.*
CASI	And to our true loves!
JANKO	To our true loves.
	They drink. CASI *again drains the glass and holds it out.* JANKO *looks at him, hesitates, then fills it again.*
CASI	And to art and poetry and theatre and joy and tolerance and gentleness and kindness and loving and laughing and dancing and singing and seeing and hearing and touching and feeling.
JANKO	Hear, hear.
	Enter EVA. *Both men are raising their glasses and about to drink when they see her.* JANKO *lowers his glass.* CASI *pauses, then drinks his glass slowly and deliberately.*
CASI	Eva. How wonderful to see you! Would you like a drink?
EVA	No thank you, Casi.
	She crosses over to him and kisses him on both cheeks.
EVA	How are you?
CASI	Well, very well.
EVA	(*Holding out her hand to* JANKO) Hello Janko, how are you?
JANKO	(*Taking her hand*) Well, very well.

52

EVA	I wasn't sure whether you would be back from Poland.
CASI	Oh we are, aren't we Janko?
JANKO	Yes, we are.
EVA	I've come over to help Constance at Liberty Hall. The struggle is going to get harder.
CASI	I'm sure it is. (*Pause*) I'm afraid we can't offer you a cup of tea. We don't make it. Nor any food, we haven't any. But you'll find Constance ministering to the poor and she'll find you something.
EVA	(*Uncertain how to take him*) I've left my bag in the hall.
CASI	Janko will see to it later.
EVA	I'll leave you then.
CASI	Naturally. That's what all you women do.
EVA	(*Frowns*) I'll see you later. Goodbye.
CASI	Perhaps. Goodbye.
	EVA *turns and starts to walk away.*
CASI	Eva!
	EVA *turns back.*
CASI	Why are you Gore-Booth women like this? It's not natural.
JANKO	Perhaps I'd better go and see if I can find us some supper.
CASI	No, stay, I need an ally.
EVA	Stay, Janko, it doesn't matter.
CASI	It doesn't matter because whatever I say won't get through to her. Or her sister.
EVA	You don't mean what you're saying now, Casi, you're drunk.
CASI	I always mean what I say when I'm drunk. I'm not drunk now. Why are you and Constance like you are?
EVA	How is that?
CASI	You don't give yourself to a man.
EVA	(*Turns away*) I'm not going to enter into that kind of discussion with you.
CASI	(*Crosses over to her, takes hold of her and swings her round to face him*) You can't give yourself to a man,

	either of you. You think Constance has given herself to me! Never! She has never let me possess her. I have lain with her, yes, I have penetrated her, she has borne me a child, but I've never possessed her.
EVA	(*Coldly*) Let me go.
CASI	(*Keeping hold*) She's not a cold woman. You are not cold. You are passionate. It was Constance's passion first drew me to her. A good, great person. None of it was ever for me. I have had her love, care, affection, comradeship. To hell with comradeship! Why, why Eva? It is so simple to give yourself to a man. I have possessed dozens of women, from prostitutes to duchesses. Under the sheets they are all the same. They abandon themselves. I take them. They want to be taken. Real women want to be taken!
	JANKO *edges away from the pair.* CASI *sees him.*
CASI	Janko, I told you not to go.
JANKO	Sir, I'm sorry, I can't stay and listen to this.
CASI	It's true what I'm saying, isn't it? You've been with women.
JANKO	Not as many as you, if you don't mind my saying so.
CASI	Enough to tell Eva I'm not lying.
EVA	(*Very quietly*) Please don't humiliate me any more.
CASI	Humiliate you! How am I humiliating you?
JANKO	Excuse me sir!
	He crosses quickly downstage where he sits, head in hands.
CASI	(*Lets* EVA *go*) How am I humiliating you? Answer me.
EVA	Is that how you treat Constance when you can't get your own way? Bully her, shout at her? Tell her she's not a proper woman? (*Pause*) Why are you saying this to me?
CASI	Because you are here and Constance is gone. I can't say it to her. I need to understand. (*Pause*) You're right, I shouldn't try to talk to you about these things. You know nothing of love, of what should happen between man and wife.

54

EVA	Do you think I live in a convent? Do you think I don't look and listen? I'm out in the world, Casi, a world you shut your eyes to. What wives tell me of their husbands is often dreadful.
CASI	Women, always women, don't you listen to the men?
EVA	I would listen to the men, but it's the women who come to fight, to take refuge, to recover themselves.
CASI	And you think they are always telling the truth? Even if they are, then perhaps their husbands are desperate because they are not getting what they need from them, what they have a right to.
EVA	You mean the right to control, to possess them completely?
CASI	That's it! That's what you can't take! You fools, you and Constance and the rest of you. Do you think I'm not possessed? If I wasn't I would have left this city for good years ago. I would never have come back. Constance is faithful in the way the world understands it, I am unfaithful, I don't deny it. But I am the one who has given up my freedom. I'm the one who's lost the sense of who he is.
EVA	You stayed because you've had fun. Because it's suited you. When it stops suiting you, you'll leave. When living with Constance becomes too difficult, you'll go.
CASI	If living with Constance is difficult, it is because she has no further need of me. I'll be in the way.
EVA	She needs you, more than she's ever needed you. To be with her. To fight with her.
CASI	To become something I cannot be. (*Pours himself another whiskey*) It's a great pity. I thought we could become something extraordinary, Constance and I. You'd better go. I won't see you later. By the time you come back I will be drunk. Goodnight.
EVA	(*Pause*) I'm sorry. Goodnight.
	She turns and walks away.
	CASI *pours himself another whiskey. Enter* CONSTANCE.

55

CONSTANCE	Casi.
CASI	I thought you'd gone! Go on! They'll be lost without you. Hurry up!
CONSTANCE	Please! Come with me. I know you're on our side. You and I together.
CASI	I told you. You and I are nothing together any more. (*Pause*) I'm going home.
CONSTANCE	But you've only just got back.
CASI	I shouldn't have. I should have stayed where I belong. It's finished for me here. I've lost you.
CONSTANCE	No! No, that's not true! I love you. You're part of me.
CASI	It's no use, Con. I need you to be with me, to think about me, to do what I want you to do. If you can't do that, we're better off without each other. (*Pause*) I don't want to be in your way.
CONSTANCE	You won't . . .
CASI	I will! I'll sulk and rage and be mean. (*Pause*) From the Ukraine, amongst my own kind, I can feel proud of you. You're a brave woman. I shall start learning to be a brave man if I'm away from you. Go!
CONSTANCE	Oh Casi, if only . . .
CASI	No. (*Pause*) I don't want to leave you for ever. Whenever I come back I'll be stronger. Go on! You know it will be better.
CONSTANCE	(*Takes his hands*) I shall miss you so much. You don't believe that. I would like you by my side in every fight.
CASI	I believe that. You're on your own, my little rebel. You will still bear my name, though. It is through you our own family will be remembered. You will give me that at least.
CONSTANCE	I shall always bear it honourably.
CASI	I know. (*He kisses her hand*) Go to your labours amongst the poor. As for me, I'm very tired. (*He kisses her hand again*) May God help you and old Ireland's cause, Madame Markiewicz. *Blackout.*

MADAME COLETTE

A play based on the life and works of Colette

'Sometimes I feel the need, sharp as thirst in summer, to know and describe. And then I pick up my pen again and begin to pin down the adjectives which dance through my thoughts like brilliant butter-flies. I soon get over it. It's only the itching of an old scar.'

This play was written for Studio 12 Theatre Company, Brighton and was performed in Brighton under the title *A Particular Intoxication* in 1983, directed by Sylvia Vickers, with the following actors, in order of appearance.

OLD COLETTE	Gillian Eddison
MELANIE	Maxine Badger
SIDO	Mary Saffrey
MINET-CHERI	Zoe Gallagher
COLETTE	Sylvia Vickers
POLAIRE	Virginia Coppins
MISSY	Christine Drummond
GIGI	Roma Downey
WILLY'S VOICE	Bernard Gallagher

Other parts were played by various members of the cast.

It was revived, under the same title but rewritten, the following year and toured East Sussex with the following cast.

OLD COLETTE	Gillian Eddison
PAULINE	Elaine Mitchell
MINET-CHERI/COLETTE	Sylvia Vickers
SIDO	Mary Saffrey
MISSY	Christine Drummond
BEL GAZOU	Virginia Coppins

Other parts played by various members of the cast.

It was performed under the present title by final year students at Guildford Drama School.

The scene is Paris in 1953. Old Colette is 80. She is confined to her bed in the Palais Royal. Her life unfolds through twelve scenes in her imagination. She is a constant presence on stage. Colette from the age of 9 to 69 is played by a different actress.

PART ONE

PROLOGUE

OLD COLETTE'S *daybed is to one side of the playing area. It is covered in red. She is sitting with her feet and legs covered by a fur rug. She remains in this position throughout the play, watching scenes played out from her past. As many props should surround her as can be gathered together – paperweights, glass walking sticks, necklaces, cases of butterflies and a crystal ball. Her bed is pushed up against a window so that she can look out over the street.* OLD COLETTE *is looking at a book of drawings of plants, birds or insects. She is using a magnifying glass. She is very still, completely concentrated on what she is looking at. After several minutes she picks up a large shell which is lying on the bed, puts it to her ear, listens intently. A delighted smile spreads across her face. She laughs aloud. She shakes the shell, listens again, laughs, lays it down, sighs. She closes her eyes for a minute or two, opens them.*

OLD COLETTE   I don't suppose you'd care much for the sea, Catkin, not yet. You could come to love it, like the others did. There have been some who walked with us every evening across the rocks, you know. Kiki used to spend most of the day staring into rock pools hoping, hoping, hoping she would see a fish. You wouldn't do that, though, not you. (*She looks around*) Where are you, you timid little thing? (*She leans right over to look under the bed*) Oh Catkin, when are you going to leave that dark safe place? Come and lie beside me – it's warm and safe on my rug too. Come on, come on! (*She straightens up*) All right, I know, cats must do things in their own good time. Nevertheless, my young friend, you've been in this room too long to cower in the corner! (*She picks up a little glass or china bell from beside the bed and rings it*) I don't know what Maurice will say when he meets you. He prefers big tough one-eyed tom cats with scars they can boast about. So you'd better start shaping up because there are only a few days until he comes back!

Enter PAULINE. *She is an elderly, comfortable, capable-looking woman.*

OLD COLETTE   Pauline, when you go to the market would you bring a little piece of haddock for this nuisance? We'll put it in the most exposed part of the room, a little every hour to keep on tempting him into the daylight. Next time you see Gabrielle, tell her I want no more kittens from that neurotic fluffball of hers. I went against all my better instincts when I said yes this time. It's poor stock, no matter who the father was. And Pauline, you can bring me some of the vegetables to prepare. I feel like doing something with my hands.

PAULINE   Hmm!

OLD COLETTE   All right, all right. I know you said so! I know I'd said so. I know that really the time for cats should be over.

PAULINE   Yes, well in the end . . . .

OLD COLETTE   It's you who looks after them. I promise you

60

	Pauline this will be the very last. If he survives at all he'll outlive me anyway! I suppose I should settle for goldfish, but I've never really been able to take to them. What's the point? Poor little things swimming round and round in a square foot of water. I'd thought about a snake, though, I thought very seriously about a snake. Very suitable for a bedridden old crone. And I could bring him out from under the blanket when I wanted to get rid of tiresome visitors.
PAULINE	If you think I'm spending half my time catching flies and looking for frogs to feed to some slimy horror you've taken a fancy to, you'd better think again. I've put up with a lot, I've shared a bath with snakes before, I've been scratched by your wild-cats, I've cleaned out whole menageries, but I've had enough, Madame Colette, I've had enough. And it's such a lovely apartment. It's such a shame to fill it with cat-trays and rabbit hutches and the like.
OLD COLETTE	No not a rabbit. I never mentioned a rabbit! No rabbits, you can rest assured.
PAULINE	Well that's one blessing. (*Pause*) You shouldn't push M. Maurice's patience too far.
OLD COLETTE	(*Pause, looks quizzically at* PAULINE, *then bursts out laughing*) Oh, Pauline. After nearly thirty years you still confuse M. Maurice with M. de Jouvenel. I suppose it's understandable. Maurices are very hard to find – he's probably the only one. He took me for precisely what I was and has never tried to change me since. A man who indulges your every whim, that's quite something. (*Pause*) Did you bring up the mail?
PAULINE	No.
OLD COLETTE	Would you mind getting it before you go to market? And just hand me my make-up and my mirror will you? I know I look dreadful this morning.

PAULINE	Are you expecting visitors?
OLD COLETTE	I'm always expecting visitors! I don't want any, not today, but if someone has made the effort to come a long way, an old friend, how can you refuse. (*Pause*) I would really like to be quiet with my thoughts this morning. Whilst the pain has stopped.
PAULINE	(*Handing over make-up*) Was it very bad last night?
OLD COLETTE	Yes. (*Looks in the mirror*) Good gracious, I knew it! What a wreck. On second thoughts, Pauline, if anyone does call, unless it's a very dear friend who can't come back, perhaps you should say I'm working. Everybody knows I work in the after-noons and during the night, so they'll realise it's a lie, but I just cannot bring myself to say I'm not well enough to see people. How can you do it? 'I'm too ill to face you.' It's an insult. Listen, when you bring the letters, I don't want bills or anything official. Nothing typed. No, that's not right, if the typing is not quite straight, if the address isn't centred and the envelope is white and square, you can bring it up.

PAULINE *exits.* OLD COLETTE *continues to apply her make-up whilst talking.*

OLD COLETTE	Would I do this I wonder if I were quite sure I'd be alone? Except for Pauline. Do I take such care just to present a reassuring face to her? Hmm. I think, I'm afraid, that it's for me. Long habit. Not want-ing to catch sight of pale eyelids, red-rimmed, eyes that don't tease any more, thin little lips lost in a parchment face. That's not the face in my mind's eye. (*Stops. Leans over to address the cat under the bed*) Animals don't know lucky they are. It's not quite fair that age doesn't chisel at their flesh in the same way. (*Pause*) Or perhaps it's just that we humans live too long. Outlive ourselves. The gradual stripping away of our grace and beauty is

just nature's way of expressing its outrage. (*Studies herself critically*) There we are. If you don't look too closely, you'd recognise the same Colette you stared at twenty, even thirty years ago. *Enter* PAULINE *with a pile of letters.* COLETTE *closes the make-up box, hands it to* PAULINE *in exchange for the letters, which she sorts through.*

OLD COLETTE   Would you just straighten the room a bit? And water the plants on the balcony, whilst I think of it. There's enough water left in the bottle without fetching more, I think. Put a drop of that stuff in it too, you know it's in a little container on the bureau. Now what are all these about? This is an interesting postmark, back of beyond, I don't know anyone in that part of France. (*She tears the envelope open rather impatiently, scans through the letter, then gives an incredulous but angry laugh*) Well if that isn't the limit! Pauline, just come and sit down for a minute and listen to this.

PAULINE *comes and sits beside her.*

OLD COLETTE   (*Reading*) Madame, I have lately been introduced to your books by an enthusiastic friend. I must confess, for my part, I found some of them rather dull, particularly your reminiscences, which were a bit 'tired' shall we say. They were also rather literary and not entirely honest. Come now, you could do better than that. Some of your works I liked better, in fact I would like to turn one or two of them into poetry, adapting your loose prose into my much tighter structure. I hope the idea appeals to you. Perhaps you would also like to write the preface. I would be grateful for any help with publication. With sincere good wishes from a fellow writer.

PAULINE   Give it to me I'll burn it in the stove. Why you have to put up with such things, I don't know. Who do they think they are, inflated bullfrogs who try to make you listen to their croaking? If it were the

	only such letter it wouldn't be so bad. But you get half a dozen a week. Give it to me!
OLD COLETTE	Don't you think I should file it? For when he sends his manuscript for the preface.
PAULINE	File it indeed! (*She snatches it*) They don't know what writing's about, these fat-bellied messieurs with their little stories and their little poems they knock off when there's nothing better to do.
OLD COLETTE	Isn't that a bit unfair?
PAULINE	No it isn't. They should ask me. I've looked after a writer for nearly forty years, I know what I'm talking about. You think because you sneak your pen and paper out quietly sometimes at two or three o'clock in the morning that I don't see what's been going on. Well, I'm the one who picks up the pieces in the morning.
OLD COLETTE	Of paper?
PAULINE	Of Madame Colette, who's fallen apart with exhaustion. I don't expect these smug smart-arses ever look like that. It's always men who criticise.
OLD COLETTE	Not always. Usually. Pauline, you're crosser than I am with this gentleman. After all he's trying to help me improve my style.
PAULINE	If I were you, I'd write him such a letter, oh yes I would. I don't know much about literature, but I know about you, and if anybody ever says anything to me about you being able to do better, and not being truthful, they'll wish they'd never opened their mouths.
OLD COLETTE	My dear, it's not worth it. Remember for every letter like that, I get the others, which would make me far too big for my boots if I were to believe a half of what they contain. (*Pause*) But I'm delighted you would be so ready to defend me.
PAULINE	Well, you so famous, over the whole world and them nothing, nothing at all!
OLD COLETTE	That's not a proper way of comparing people. Give

	me the letter back, it shall not be burned. You must examine every criticism to see if there is not a grain of truth in it.
PAULINE	(*Gets up and hands letter back*) That's put me in a right mood to haggle with the stall holders. You'll get your fish for rock bottom price today, I can tell you.
OLD COLETTE	(*Laughing*) Splendid. By the way, I finished the chocolates last night, will you bring me another box? Not the same, I'd like a change. Those coffee creams you bought last time were splendid.
PAULINE	I didn't buy them, they were out of your stock. You still have a stack of boxes from your birthday.
OLD COLETTE	Have I? I get through them so quickly, I was sure they must be all gone by now.
PAULINE	You get sent them so often, I don't always tell you. It's not a good thing!
OLD COLETTE	Bless my soul, the woman's rationing my chocolates! Perhaps you're right – I was going to ask you to get me a box right now as I have some, but perhaps it would be better for me to wait until you come back. You bring them when you bring the fish.
PAULINE	(*Eyeing the mail suspiciously*) I hope you don't have any more insults in that lot.
OLD COLETTE	I can see I'll have to be more careful what I read to you in future.
PAULINE	You wouldn't have read it to me if M. Maurice had been around, you'd have read it to him. I keep my ears open though, I take it all in. I won't be long. If I were you I'd have a little nap whilst I'm gone.
OLD COLETTE	Perhaps I will.
PAULINE	I don't want M. Maurice to find you looking peaky. You've got to start building yourself up.
OLD COLETTE	Funny, that's what I said to the kitten.
PAULINE	It's good advice. I'll get you some haddock as well.
OLD COLETTE	Please don't. (*As* PAULINE *prepares to leave*) Don't forget to bring me the vegetables.

PAULINE	No. You don't have to tell me everything three times. My memory's not going yet.
	Exit PAULINE. COLETTE *lies back her eyes closed for a minute, very tired. She sits up and looks at the other letters.*
OLD COLETTE	This one could be interesting. It's from America, Connecticut, so it could well be from a dear lady who looked after me and Maurice when we went to New York. She lives in Connecticut now. Much more appropriate. She had a country bloom about her, wonderful golden eyes. And she transformed her miserable little city studio into a country garden with blossoms and plants and pine cones and bowls of fruit everywhere. So I hope it's from her, because I liked her, I liked her a lot. You don't often come across that kind of freshness. (*She opens the letter, reads it*) Good gracious! (*She continues to read*) Her daughter! Her daughter a grown up person writing to me! Surely not, why it's only a few years ago that she sent me a photo. (*She does a mental calculation*) Well I never, that's right, she would be twenty-two now. I never thought of her as growing up. So! This young lady from Connecticut is not only grown up, she is writing a thesis – I know it's a nasty word, and we don't like it at all, but there's nothing else for it – this serious-minded American Miss is writing a thesis on me and my work. Is coming to Paris, wants to see me if she may. She realises how busy I am and all that, but it would be such an honour etc. She wants to get to the heart of my work, she wants to meet the real Colette. No, she doesn't say that, I do. (*She puts the letter down*) Oh dear, oh dear, oh dear. I will not sit po-faced for hours talking about 'my work'. What can I say? But I'll see her for her mother's sake. If she looks like her mother at least I shall have the pleasure that only the company of a truly beautiful woman can give. But I shall not

speak in that dry intellectual way that is expected
of me. I shall not 'explain' my books. I shall tell
her . . . I shall tell her to think of her mother, that's
what she must do. That's the clue, the key to it all.
That's where it starts, for her, for me. With a
mother. (*To audience*) The face of an otter with
invisible whiskers. They were there all right, the
whiskers, twitching, testing the air. Sitting in an
enchanted garden, which nuzzled up to a cold
stone house, covering its bones with leaves and
spiders' webs. We had wisteria as a lintel for the
back door, and the garden gate was long since lost
in the boughs of an old laburnum. This was my
mother's kingdom, glowing through the year with
her beloved purples and reds. The crimson flush of
my childhood. (*She looks out over the audience, as
if seeing her past*)

SCENE 1. The Garden

SIDO *comes in, settles downstage. She is carrying
a sewing box and some material.*

OLD COLETTE   Sido, my mother, used to sit on the wooden steps
leading down to the tangle of wild grasses which
could hardly be called a 'lawn'. On every step
were pots of seedlings. Winter and summer alike
she kept them under tender care . . .

SIDO   (*Calling*) Minet-Chéri (*Pause*) Minet-Chéri. Come
here immediately. It's no good keeping as quiet as
a hedge sparrow, I can see you in the
currant bushes. I said *now*, Minet-Chéri.

OLD COLETTE   I always obeyed her in the end. I knew her sharp
eyes saw everything.
Enter COLETTE *as* MINET-CHERI. *She comes
across reluctantly to her mother. She has
characteristic long plaits with a broad ribbon tied
round her head.*

67

SIDO	I hope you haven't been eating the plums (*Looks sharply at her*) All right. I don't want to hear a word if you have colic, you know what I told you, you know what might happen. Don't expect any sympathy. Sit beside me. MINET-CHERI *sits. She begins to look at the flower pots.*
SIDO	Don't touch those flowers pots! You'll injure the plants.
MINET-CHERI	But maman, there's nothing in them.
SIDO	How do you know?
MINET-CHERI	I can't see anything.
SIDO	To think the girl's been brought up in a garden. All these pots have seeds in them, tiny germs of life curled up under the soil. They're sleeping. Don't disturb them.
MINET-CHERI	Maman, those caterpillars have eaten nearly all the cabbages.
SIDO	And so?
MINET-CHERI	Why didn't you let Achille and me pick them off and drown them?
SIDO	And who are you and Achille to play at being gods, taking life in your hands?
MINET-CHERI	They were only caterpillars.
SIDO	You are only a little girl.
MINET-CHERI	Little girls are better than caterpillars.
SIDO	Indeed? Who says so?
MINET-CHERI	The priest for a start.
SIDO	You should know better than to quote the priest to me. A priest who sends dogs out of the church. You know how perfectly behaved my dog is. 'But he growled during the sermon, madame'. That just shows his good sense. I would like to growl during the sermon. Caterpillars have a right to exist just like you.
MINET-CHERI	(*Muttering*) So do cabbages.
SIDO	That's enough. You should be employing your time more usefully at your age than running

	around the vegetables killing harmless creatures.
	It's time you learnt to sew.
MINET-CHERI	To sew!
SIDO	That's what I said. Haven't you washed your ears this morning?
MINET-CHERI	But we have sewing lessons at school.
SIDO	And what have you made?
MINET-CHERI	I haven't finished anything yet.
SIDO	Why not?
MINET-CHERI	We've started lots of different things.
SIDO	Eugénie's mother was showing me all the napkins, the cushion covers her daughter had made for her. She's in your class. She's finished everything.
MINET-CHERI	I'm no good at sewing, Maman.
SIDO	You never will be if you don't do it. It's a disgrace at your age. I've tacked this cloth for you. Let me see you hem it in neat little stitches.

She hands the cloth to MINET-CHERI, *who takes it very reluctantly. She then hands her the needle and thread.* MINET-CHERI *then makes several attempts to thread the needle under mother's stern gaze. She then starts to tie a knot in the end of the thread.*

SIDO	No knots! A double stitch, no knots.

Laboriously MINET-CHERI *begins to sew.*

SIDO	Good heavens, child what great spiders legs you're making!

They both begin to laugh. SIDO *strokes* MINET-CHERI'S *forehead and tucks stray strands of hair back under her ribbon.*

Try again. I have ten minutes before I must go up and brush your sister's hair. Goodness knows who'll do it when she's married.

MINET-CHERI	Perhaps she'll cut it.
SIDO	Don't say such dreadful things.
MINET-CHERI	But why not? You've said yourself it's a curse to have such a tent of long black hair down to the floor.

69

SIDO	That hair isn't hers to cut. It's mine. I've looked after it all these years, like yours. You'll never cut your hair without my permission, so you'll never cut it.
MINET-CHERI	Maman . . .
SIDO	Yes? What does this little tone of voice mean?
MINET-CHERI	Is Juliette expecting? Is that why she's getting married?
SIDO	What fantasies the child has! How do you think she'd be expecting?
MINET-CHERI	Like anybody else.
SIDO	Well think again. How could she be, when they have seen each other for no more than a few times, with everyone around them looking on? How stupid you look Minet-Chéri, with your mouth and eyes open like that. You're prettier when you look stupid. It's a pity you look so intelligent most of the time. Let me have a look at your stitches. (*She examines* MINET-CHERI'S *stitching*) They're better but they could be even smaller too. *She hands the cloth back.* MINET-CHERI *begins to sew again. There is a pause whilst* SIDO *looks out at the garden and breathes in the smell of the earth.*
MINET-CHERI	Maman . . .
SIDO	(*Distractedly*) Mmm?
MINET-CHERI	I'm glad Juliette's not expecting. I'm glad she won't have to suffer just yet.
SIDO	(*Sharply*) Suffer! What do you mean?
MINET-CHERI	Oh maman, all the blood, all dirty and horrid!
SIDO	You've been reading that book by Zola again, haven't you! What does Monsieur Zola know about childbirth? I've read that description, it's not like that. You forget the pain. I was in pain for three days and nights with you. But I never regretted it. They say that the babies like you, which are carried so high are the dearest, because they were closest to their mother's hearts. Look

70

	Minet-Chéri, look at that blackbird! What a handsome fellow. Look how he's using his claws to hold the fruit.
MINET-CHERI	What about the scarecrow?
SIDO	(*Laughing*) Oh that doesn't bother him to be sure! Look at the proud little head. See how he only goes for the best ones too?
MINET-CHERI	(*On the point of tears*) But maman, all those lovely cherries!
SIDO	(*Turns to her daughter*) So what?
	MINET-CHERI *begins to snivel.*
SIDO	(*In sudden realisation, putting her arms round her*) Of course! I forgot! Little girls like cherries too.
	MINET-CHERI *exits,* SIDO *sits on steps looking at the garden.*
OLD COLETTE	Little girls have no more claim to ripe cherries than a cheeky blackbird. No more no less. So Sido saved some for me and let the blackbird choose his daily breakfast. There was enough in the garden for us all. Nature and Sido worked in harmony – no tightlipped pruning for our apple trees, no geometric borders cleansed of what other people call weeds, all the plants were taught to live side by side respecting each other's right to air and sunshine. I wonder how carefully this daughter of Connecticut has read my books? I wonder if she remembers my mother's letter in *Break of Day*? It is so important, that letter, so important. She was writing to Henry. Henry de Jouvenel, a good name at any rate.
SIDO	(*Stands up*) Dear Sir, You have invited me to spend a fortnight with you and my beloved daughter. You who are so close to her realise how seldom I see her, what pleasure I find in her company and I am touched by the invitation. However, I must decline, at least for the time being, for this reason: my pink cactus is likely to flower. It's a very rare

71

plant. When it was given to me I was told that in our climate it would only flower once every few years. Now, I'm a very old woman and if I went away whilst my cactus was in bloom I would certainly never see it flower. Thank you once more. With much love and deep regret, Yours, Sidonie Colette.

She exits.

OLD COLETTE She was seventy-six when she wrote that. She died the following year. (*Long pause*) Dear me, it's a morning for going back is it? Reviewing my life? Again? It's Connecticut's fault. And maybe the fault of our patronising poet too. 'Not entirely honest' he said. Perhaps he's right, perhaps I've not always been entirely honest. We always want to protect someone. Ourselves, of course, but other people too. When I got married for the first time, pretending to be such a grown-up lady when I was so young, pretending that I could leave my garden, my village and live in Paris, because I was with a very special man, a man of the world, twice my age, who would take me to champagne parties where I would meet the most brilliant and famous people of the day, and I wasn't being honest. It was a convincing lie after all what country girl wouldn't be entranced by the idea of Paris in the 1890s? And to be introduced as the wife of a famous music critic who knew everyone, was more than I could ever have dreamed. Yet there were misgivings locked away firmly behind the excitement. Sido never said a word as she looked across the table at me on my wedding day, but she knew.

SCENE 2. Paris

Enter COLETTE. *She is now in her early twenties. She moves around the stage listlessly. Her whole*

72

	demeanour should indicate exhaustion. Finally she sits hunched over her stomach, a picture of misery.
SIDO	So!
COLETTE	Maman!
SIDO	What a charming apartment your husband has brought you to. You can hardly see your hand in front of your face. Good gracious, what's this on the walls?
COLETTE	Confetti. The previous tenant put it there. It's very difficult to scrape off. You get quite fond of it.
SIDO	Does the stove always make such a bad smell?
COLETTE	We've had it looked at, they say there's nothing wrong. The fumes might be getting me down, though, don't you think?
SIDO	(*Gives her a long look*) Oh my dear, why didn't you tell me?
COLETTE	(*Her voice begins to tremble*) I'm all right, maman, really.
	She begins to cry.
SIDO	Oh, my poor dear. (*She crosses over and hugs* COLETTE *to her, rocking her like a baby*) You should have told me. All those lies. I thought you'd grown out of telling lies.
COLETTE	(*Putting her arms around her mother's neck*) It's not as bad as you think.
SIDO	Isn't it? Where is Monsieur Willy at this moment?
COLETTE	Why he's at his office. He has to work long hours. It's not his fault. He looks after me as well as he can.
SIDO	I should have known. I did know, that's what's so dreadful. I knew but I couldn't say anything. You wouldn't have listened.
COLETTE	I love him. He loves me. He takes me to concerts, to the theatre, everywhere. Maman, we meet such distinguished people. It's just that I haven't fitted in yet to the way of life in Paris. People live at night in Paris, maman.
SIDO	And the rest of the time? When the sun is shining

	in the Bois de Boulogne – oh yes I know my Paris – you are stuck in here on your own.
COLETTE	Not on my own maman, I have a lovely angora cat Kiki-la-Doucette. She's a darling. She's around somewhere. Kiki, come out and meet maman.
SIDO	An angora cat is not sufficient company, even for a Colette!
COLETTE	People call on me sometimes.
SIDO	When did you last have a good meal?
COLETTE	I've had a stomach upset recently. I haven't felt like eating.
SIDO	You've grown so thin Minet-Chéri. It does not suit you.
COLETTE	It's quite fashionable now, though. A friend of Willy's, an actress, has a sixteen-inch waist.
SIDO	We have never had sixteen-inch waists in our family. We do not come from a race of greyhounds. Tell me truthfully, don't you like married life?
COLETTE	(*Not quite sure what she means*) I like most of it. Yes, I like it.
SIDO	I mean don't you like sharing your bed with a husband?
COLETTE	(*After a moment's hesitation*) It is comforting to lie with my head on his shoulder next to his big warm body. I think it wouldn't be as reassuring if he were little and thin.
SIDO	(*Relentlessly*) And the other thing?
COLETTE	Oh maman!
	She shrugs her shoulders and looks away. Long pause.
SIDO	Is he unfaithful?
COLETTE	How can you suggest it?
SIDO	If he isn't he will be. My first husband was like that. Drank a lot and couldn't keep his hands off women.
COLETTE	Willy isn't like that, he works very hard. He's highly respected and everyone knows him.
SIDO	For one reason or another. I'll say no more. Minet-

	Chéri your hair is in a dreadful state. How long is it since you washed it? It doesn't matter. I shall stay for a while to get you back into condition.
COLETTE	You can't, what about Papa, the animals, the garden?
SIDO	They'll be all right. They're all well. They'll all be all right.
COLETTE	(*After a pause*) I don't know whether Willy will think it's a good idea.
SIDO	Does M. Willy think it's a good idea to leave his wife to pine away until he doesn't have a wife any more?
COLETTE	It's not a very big apartment. You'd feel so cooped up.
SIDO	(*Gives her daughter a long look*) Are you afraid of your husband Minet-Chéri? My Minet-Chéri was never frightened of anything.
COLETTE	(*Lowers her eyes*) He's still like a stranger. How long will it be before we're friends? When we wrote to each other when we were engaged, he seemed like my best friend ever. I could write anything to that good kind uncle Willy. Maman, I was sure marriage would be so much more, not less. (*She bursts into tears*) Oh maman, I do love him so, how can I get near him?
SIDO	(*Stroking her forehead*) You can't, because he'll never get near you! My little fox terrier once trotted around for months after a bulldog until she came in season and he tried to do what any male dog would. That was the end of that.
COLETTE	(*Begins to laugh*) Maman, you are absurd! *They kiss and hug each other and* SIDO *exits.*
OLD COLETTE	When you're very lonely, cut off from everything that has been your strength, the feel of earth, the smell of flowers, it almost needs a miracle to bring you round. But Sido did it, when she went home I was almost well again.
COLETTE	(*Sits up cheerfully*) Dear Maman, Today was so

lovely that the Bois de Boulogne blossomed with
the taffetas, silks and velvets of riders and dog
walkers. Such gaiety. I wore the new tartan skirt
with the ruffles you gave me and felt so fine. I
don't know whether it's a good or bad thing that it
no longer falls off me. I rather enjoyed being pale
and elegant, I'm sure it will never happen again.
Kiki has been sulking like mad since you left. It's
quite clear that the moment she set eyes on you she
preferred you to me. She sends you three meows
and a prolonged purr. Willy has offered to buy me
a poodle for my birthday but I don't think I could
live up to a poodle. I must learn to be much more
Parisienne. I'm sure it wouldn't like my accent.
I've noticed that Willy's lady friends' poodles gaze
at me in astonishment when I speak. 'My dear,
those r's. Is it possible? Does anyone really speak
like that?' 'I know, darling, imagine if one fell into
the hands of such a mistress the shame of it, every
time she opened her mouth. Not even a jewelled
collar would make up for it. Not that she could
afford a jewelled collar. Oh, the very idea makes
my tail tremble, what a lucky escape, not belong-
ing to her.' Willy sends you his love,

OLD COLETTE He didn't, of course, so I still lied a little. M. Willy
never gave Madame Sidonie Colette a thought
once she'd cleared off out of his dark little flat. I
don't think he thought about me that much either
except when I was looking at him with big mourn-
ful eyes, wondering why I'd got myself into this
trap and how on earth I could get myself out of it.
It was when I was giving him that whipped-spaniel
gaze over croissants one morning that he suggested
we go home for a bit, my home, my village, visit
my old friends, my old school. It was a kind
gesture, I thought. I hadn't yet realised how much
Willy liked schoolgirls. How stupid of me. It was a
schoolgirl he married, he wanted her sense of fun

76

restored by the smell of ink and chalk, he wanted his own desire revived by nubile adolescents in uniforms.

COLETTE Dear Maman, We did so enjoy our visit. I was surprised how interested Willy was in seeing my school and meeting my teachers. He laughed until tears ran down his cheeks over some of the stories I told him about the things we got up to. It was very gratifying to be able to entertain the distinguished monsieur in that way, especially when I've seen him very bored at the theatre. He even said I ought to write it all down, that it might make an interesting book. He'll help me. He's used to writers. Lots of them work for him in some way or other, I'm never quite sure how. Your daughter is going to turn author!

SCENE 3. Writing

She sits at a desk, head in hands. She hears the following voices on tape as she sits.

WILLEY'S VOICE Four hours work my dear, four hours no less. I'll unlock the door in four hours time. Discipline is what a writer needs. Don't be afraid to spice it up a bit, that's what the public wants.

WOMAN'S VOICE I thought you ought to know, madame (*fades*)

WILLY'S VOICE Not asleep yet, my pet? You mustn't stay awake for newspaper men they work so late!

WOMAN'S VOICE It's a scandal that such an innocent as you should be so shamefully treated by such a man!

WILLY'S VOICE Another exercise book full already! Well done my pigeon! We'll put it in this drawer with the first.

WOMAN'S VOICE If madame were to go to number fifty, rue Bochard, Saron at 3 pm on Wednesday afternoon.

WILLY'S VOICE Don't bother to meet me tonight my love, I have an urgent deadline.

WOMAN'S VOICE	3 pm on Wednesday afternoon, 50 rue Bochard, Saron.
WILLY'S VOICE	Just an actress I met through my work, dear heart.
WOMAN'S VOICE	3 pm Wednesday afternoon.
SECOND WOMAN'S VOICE	(*Gives a loud shriek*) Ah! Who the hell are you? Bloody cheek. Get out of here. Fuck off!
WILLY'S VOICE	Lotte Kinceler, my dear. Lotte, my wife Colette.
SECOND WOMAN'S VOICE	Jesus Christ, just what the fuck do you think you're doing Willy?
	There is a jumble of voices repeating the same phrases over again.
WILLY'S VOICE	Another exercise book!
WOMAN'S VOICE	3 pm Wednesday afternoon.
SECOND WOMAN'S VOICE	What the fuck do you think you're doing Willy?
	(COLETTE *puts her hands over her ears. She gets up, starts to touch her toes. She goes through a whole routine of movements and mime exercises. This may well be accompanied by taped music from the 1890 period. At last she sits again, reads through what she's written.*
COLETTE	The washroom was sparsely furnished with a large zinc covered table, 8 bowls, 8 bars of soap, eight pairs of towels, 8 sponges were aligned, all exactly alike. The linen was marked with indelible ink. It was all very neat and clean.
	I asked 'Do you have baths?'
	'Oh yes, that's great fun. The water's heated up in one of those big vats they put grapes in. It's as big as a whole room. We all take our clothes off and get in to wash ourselves.'
	'With no clothes on?'
	'How could we get washed with clothes on? Rose Raquenet doesn't like it of course, because she's too thin. If you saw her, she's nothing but skin and bones and her chest is flat like a boy's. Now Jousse, on the other hand, is like a woman with a

baby, they're as big as this. And that girl who wears a night cap, you know, Poisson, she's covered in hair everywhere like a bear and she's got a blue bum.'

'What do you mean blue ?'

'Blue, like you are when it's freezing cold.'

'Charming!'

'No, really, if I were a boy I wouldn't relish having a bath with her.'

She crosses words out and begins writing. There is the sound of steps on the stairs, a key turning in the lock. She leans back stretches herself like a cat, stands up shakes herself.

COLETTE   Willy! At last.

OLD COLETTE I spiced it up but Willy didn't read it for two years. When he did, he spiced it up some more, published it four years later and it was a success. 'Claudine at School' by M. Willy appealed to the Parisian taste. It was made into a play, with his mistress of the moment, Polaire, playing the part. She and I would appear together as the Claudine twins. We were trailed round the cafés, shown off in the Bois de Boulogne. I had to cut my hair. My mother was deeply shocked.

SCENE 4. *Claudine*

COLETTE *takes off her long plait, puts on a hat. Enter* POLAIRE, *who comes to stand behind her, the same clothes the same hair. They stand be side then begin the Claudine Song and Dance routine.*

COLETTE   Sweet sixteen, full of grace
          Laughing eyes, painted face.

POLAIRE   Neat little arse, scarcely ripe
          Don't try it on, I'm not that type!

COLETTE   Life's all fun even at school
          Love and let love is our rule.

POLAIRE	She loves me, I love him
	What a game! Keeps you slim!
BOTH	We're Willy's twins, the Claudine girls
TOGETHER	Neat little pinnies, bouncing curls,
	We walk out on his arm
	One on each side,
	We succumb to his charm
	Swallow our pride,
	We're just good friends, nothing more
	None of that, you can be sure.
	They stop. Kiss each other on the cheek four times.
COLETTE	How are you Polaire?
POLAIRE	A little tired my dear Colette. How are you?
COLETTE	Very well.
POLAIRE	I hope I haven't given M. Willy my cold. The poor dear will insist on carrying on as usual even though I told him he would be ill. Such a lusty man!
COLETTE	Indeed. How are the houses?
POLAIRE	Wonderful my dear. They do love me so. I'm still getting hundreds of letters to Claudine. Some of them are very embarrassing. Many are from women, you know.
COLETTE	You surprise me.
POLAIRE	Oh no I don't. I should pass them on to you – you are the model, you could probably read their suggestions without blushing. You told M. Willy all those dreadful things that went on at your school.
COLETTE	I told you M. Willy has a fine imagination. My schooldays were not at all what you think.
POLAIRE	Still you don't mind women, do you? It doesn't make you sick that half the people in the cafés think we're lovers.
COLETTE	Well, you wouldn't be a lover to be ashamed of Polaire.
POLAIRE	Oh it's disgusting, stop it!
COLETTE	How is Pierre?
POLAIRE	Pierre is a brute! But oh Colette, what a magnificent brute. He will kill me in the end, I know it.

	What a way to go!
COLETTE	I couldn't help noticing the bruise below your ear. You've covered it well don't worry but I have sharp eyes.
POLAIRE	There are more bruises where you can't see. What can I do? My legs just fall apart when he comes into the room. You know what I mean?
COLETTE	No, Polaire, I do not know what you mean.
POLAIRE	Oh well, chacun à son gout, I suppose. Come on, our manager is waiting, dear.
	She trots out COLETTE *gazes after her with mixed amusement and sadness. She sighs, shakes herself, exits.*
OLD COLETTE	Willy knew a winner when he'd got one all right. Four hours forced labour a day produced *Claudine at School*, *Claudine in Paris*, *Claudine Married*, *The Innocent Wife*, all published under Willy's name.
	There is a knock at the door. Without waiting for reply, PAULINE *comes in. She has a box of chocolates, a cup of coffee and some vegetables to prepare.*
PAULINE	A cup of coffee, a box of chocolates and a pound of carrots.
OLD COLETTE	You remembered the fish?
PAULINE	Of course, it's cooking.
OLD COLETTE	He might have preferred it raw.
PAULINE	You don't want pieces of raw fish lying around stinking the place out do you?
OLD COLETTE	Fish doesn't stink unless it's off. I hope it isn't off?
PAULINE	It's as fresh as a bunch of violets. Do you think I'd buy rotten fish? It's cooking now whether he would have preferred it fresh or not.
OLD COLETTE	Oh dear, don't get in a mood, have a chocolate. Oh go on. Sit down for a bit, have a chocolate and tell me about the market.
PAULINE	(*Sits, takes a chocolate*) You don't want to know about the market, you're only trying to get round me.

OLD COLETTE	Do I need to?
PAULINE	I haven't been able to get that letter out of my mind. I hope you've been writing back and telling him where to get off.
OLD COLETTE	No, I've been thinking about other things. The daughter of an American friend wants to come to see me, to interview me about my work.
PAULINE	I hope you're going to say no.
OLD COLETTE	I haven't decided.
PAULINE	They don't want to know about your work, they just want to boast about meeting Madame Colette, seeing her apartment, shaking her hand. They tire you out.
OLD COLETTE	She's very polite. And she's already a graduate. We must respect scholarship Pauline, take it seriously.
PAULINE	Scholarship, fiddlesticks.
OLD COLETTE	Indeed, I'm inclined to agree with you. But we mustn't say it too loudly.
PAULINE	You didn't have to go to university to know what you know.
OLD COLETTE	Perhaps I would have been better off going to university than marrying M. Willy. Not that I had the chance. If I'd been able to become a Bachelor of Arts I might have understood a bit more of the world.
PAULINE	Huh! You don't learn that from books!
OLD COLETTE	I hope you might. Don't put down books Pauline, we owe our good standard of living to them, you and I.
PAULINE	I don't mean your books, I mean those books, the ones they read at university.
OLD COLETTE	The wouldn't have taught me to beware of M. Willy?
PAULINE	Not a chance.
OLD COLETTE	Perhaps you're right. Can you imagine it Pauline, you with your solid, reliable man beside you, what it was like to live with a rake? Not a semi-

82

	respectable bon bourgeois who sets up a little woman on the side, but a full-blooded, unashamed libertine. A man who thought it was quite all right to bring his mistress home. The first time it was awful, you should have seen my prudish face! She prodded about looking at things, her blouse unbuttoned, talking about what she did and didn't like in bed.
PAULINE	I don't know how you put up with it for so long.
OLD COLETTE	Nor do I now. Thirteen years. Thirteen years living together and not together.
PAULINE	I wouldn't do it.
OLD COLETTE	You might if you loved him.
PAULINE	How could you love a man like that? You only have to look at his photo to see what he was like.
OLD COLETTE	His photos don't do him justice. They all make him look like a pear. They don't catch the look in his eye, no camera could do that. I wasn't the only one to come under his spell, he was wildy attractive even though he wasn't handsome.
PAULINE	That's all very well to be swept off your feet when you're young. But to let yourself be treated like that, to go on loving him in spite of everything!
OLD COLETTE	Perhaps I didn't. It's hard to tell, it's a long time ago. Anyway, where would I have gone if I'd left him, how would I have lived? Back to mother? No, too much pride.
PAULINE	Don't ask me. All I know is I'd rather starve than go through what you went through. You could have got a place in a good family as a governess. I don't know, anything. I would have done.
OLD COLETTE	(*Pause*) You're right, I lacked courage. Have another chocolate.
PAULINE	No thank you, I'd better go down and see to that fish. (*She gets up*) I wish you wouldn't talk to me about your first husband it upsets me. *Exits.*
OLD COLETTE	(*To audience*) It's all very well for Pauline, she was

brought up to be practical. But I'm no good at any of the things you need to be employed as any kind of servant. A governess! I'd have been hopeless! Anyway I had a sort of job with Willy. I was one of his ghost writers. I didn't imagine I could exist as an author in my own right. In the end he made it possible. He pushed me out, but he made it possible for me to earn a living without him, before he closed the door on me. I bet you'd never think I'd been a dancer, eh? Not to look at me now with these useless little legs. I have to be content with dancing with the head and hands. When I was young, I danced. Willy made me a performer. He sent me for private dance and mime lessons with one of France's best known artistes, what do you think of that? And classes at the Mimi Pinson School of Modern Pantomime.

SCENE 5. The Mime Class

Enter members of the company, including
COLETTE. *They go through the routine of a mime class, then exit.*

OLD COLETTE   (*To audience*) I think I should talk to Miss Connecticut about the mime. She'll like that. What a time that was! When the century was still very young. A time to make a new start, try new adventures. I wonder. I wonder how much I should tell a well brought-up young woman, even in 1952, about what we did in 1905? What shall I tell her about the next protector to whom I turned when my marriage foundered. Will she understand? Will she even want to know? The daughters of America will surely not want to know about one of the most notorious ridiculed women of Gay Paree. And yet she should have been received in every salon in Europe, her name was impressive enough –

madame la Marquise de Belbeuf, daughter of the
Duc de Morny, niece of Napoleon III, great-grand-
daughter of the Empress Josephine, known to her
friends as 'Missy'. (*She leans back*)

SCENE 6. The Lesbian Party

Enter the company. As many women as are avail-
able should take part in the scene wearing various
pieces of men's clothing. COLETTE *is dressed in a*
complete evening suit, but made up. MISSY *is not*
made up. She is extremely masculine. She is stiff,
awkward and shy. She and COLETTE *are stand-*
ing talking quietly. MISSY *offers* COLETTE *a*
cigar which she takes. MISSY *lights it up for her,*
takes one herself, lights it. The other women are
all well-born, defiantly arrogant.

BARONESS	(*To Lady L*) I don't care what you say, my love, it's important to keep one's husband in a good humour. They can make life very difficult if they choose. Yours has been a perfect lamb until now.
LADY L	Nobody was more surprised than I was when he exploded.
BARONESS	What do you expect if you are out every single night?
LADY L	So what? So is he.
BARONESS	Irrelevant. Just once in a while he should find you waiting for him in bed. For him always to be in first, what a disgrace.
LADY L	What do you mean, in bed?
BARONESS	In bed, my sweetheart, showing a bit of tit.
LADY L	What on earth for?
BARONESS	To show you're still his wife.
LADY L	He doesn't want me, what are you talking about?
BARONESS	You must still show you're available. That's diplomacy.
LADY L	And if he avails himself?

BARONESS	Lie back and think of France.
LADY L	Ugh! I couldn't! I've got right out of the habit.
COLETTE	(*Laughing*) My dears, you'd better stop there or Missy won't know where to put herself.
BARONESS	She never does! That's her problem.
LADY L	Now don't tease her, Nounou. It's not fair. Missy is a perfect gentleman and I wouldn't have her otherwise. So she's shy, aren't you dear? It's a pity there aren't more shy people around. Everyone these days is far too crude. You certainly are. Do you know, I was quite innocent until I started talking to you.
BARONESS	Me! I'm modesty incarnate beside some of our friends. Have you ever had a private conversation with Renée, for example?
LADY L	Does one have private conversations with Renée? I thought it was impossible to get a conversation going at all. She's always flitting about looking half dead, or half cut. I was supposed to have dinner at her place the other day. My God, I thought, does she eat? I mean she's like a wisp of straw she's so thin and brittle. I'd never been round there before. How can one live with the curtains drawn and the windows closed and that choking incense burning everywhere? I thought we'd get a Chinese cracker and some jasmine tea and that would be that. Oh no, when my eyes got used to the gloom I saw the most splendid feast, lobsters, pâté de foie gras, pheasants, everything. The best champagne too. Is it possible to eat like this and look like that, I asked myself. Of course she didn't eat. There she was in a long black evening dress, hair falling all over the place, drugged up to the eyeballs, all ready to leave! 'I'm so sorry' she said. 'I have to go. She's sent for me. I have to go. She won't leave me alone. Enjoy yourselves.' And off she went.
BARONESS	You're lucky not to have seen what she got up to

	next. These two apparently go in for some extraordinary practices.
LADY L	But her poetry's so vague, so romantic.
COLETTE	Never confuse what an author writes with what she does.
BARONESS	In other words, my precious, authors are hypocrites. The more they appear to reveal themselves in their writing the more hypocritical they are.
MISSY	That's not what she said.
LADY L	No it isn't. You're very naughty to suggest our lovely Colette is a hypocrite. COLETTE *steps forward, takes off her jacket and tie, runs her fingers through her hair.*
LADY L	After all, she's one of us.
BARONESS	Is she?
LADY L	She's Missy's little friend!
MISSY	Hush. None of you knows her. She's not one of you. She has discretion.
BARONESS	We all have that when receiving my dear. You should see me at my soirées, perfect hostess, dressed in the latest fashion, wearing the family diamonds to the manner born.
LADY L	Well you are, aren't you baroness?
BARONESS	What?
LADY L	To the manner born?
BARONESS	Quite so! By the way, Missy, did you see Bibi's new arab mare this morning? Cute little thing. Well let-down fetlocks. Lot of spirit.
LADY L	Like Bibi.
BARONESS	Yes they made a very pretty pair. She knows what suits her. I swear she half chose that horse to match her chestnut curls. I'd take either of them if they were offered.
LADY L	When are you going to get a little pony, Colette?
BARONESS	Little pony! She's not a child.
LADY L	But she's a beginner, isn't she? And she's not very big. Do you ride at all, my dear?

COLETTE	Only a bike.
LADY L	A bike (*Shrieks with laughter*) Good heavens, a bike!

LADY L *and the* BARONESS *both go off into fits of giggles and do an imitation of* COLETTE *riding a bike whilst the other rides a horse.*

MISSY	Come, Colette, I want to ask your opinion about a painting I've bought in the dining room. Excuse us, for a moment. (*She bows slightly*)

MISSY *and* COLETTE *move away from stage centre as if off stage.*

LADY L	Come up and see my etchings, darling!
BARONESS	Discretion! She may have discretion but if so why does that pig of a husband, or about-to-be ex-husband, or whatever he is, behave in that way? She must have told him a thing or two to inspire that kind of spite? Mind you it was quite funny.
LADY L	What do you mean?
BARONESS	You mean you haven't heard? I thought all Paris knew. Where have you been hiding yourself?
LADY L	No. Go on, tell me.
BARONESS	That terrible M. Willy was riding about on trains to and from the suburbs all yesterday in 'Ladies Only' compartments. Every time a guard got on and challenged him, he replied 'But Monsieur, I have every right to be here. I am one of the greatest ladies in France, I am Missy, the marquise de Belbeuf. All Paris knows I look like a man.'
LADY L	(*Collapses in giggles*) Oh how dreadful! What a terrible man.

They move out of the stage area, still arm in arm, giggling.

COLETTE *and* MISSY *come across to stage centre again.*

COLETTE	I'm so sorry. What a pig he is!
MISSY	It doesn't matter.
COLETTE	Why should he hurt you like that? He has no right. No reason.

MISSY	He has a reason. Outrage. He has turned from an indulgent husband to an outraged husband.
COLETTE	He's hardly my husband any more. It was his suggestion we go our separate ways.
MISSY	You're not divorced. What you do still reflects on him. I understand.
COLETTE	What nonsense! It's absolutely unforgivable. I shall ...
MISSY	(*Cutting in*) You will do nothing my dear. (*Pause*) Except what you are already doing. That is enough, more than enough. (COLETTE *tries to speak*) No. I want to hear no more about M. Willy. I thought we were going to rehearse? If we're really going through with this we'll need all the practice we can get.
COLETTE	Yes we're going through with it. Especially now. Now more than ever. Let's get ready. *They exit.*
OLD COLETTE	(*To audience*) I'm not sure now why we wanted to do it. More out of a drive to shock than for love of the theatre, I suppose. Missy was no author and even less of a performer, but the two of us put on a show which created the biggest sensation of my whole life. The catcalls were deafening. The only applause was from Willy, perverse as ever.

SCENE 7. *The Pantomime*

Enter one of the company as SHOWGIRL, *the others, as audience, sit near* OLD COLETTE.

SHOWGIRL	And now ladies and gentlemen, the Moulin Rouge proudly presents a two act pantomime by Mme la Marquise de Belbeuf (*whistles from the audience*) entitled 'The Egyptian Dream' starring Colette Willy (*Whistles*) and a brilliant newcomer Yssim (*Laughter and disturbance*). *The showgirl flounces off. The music becomes*

89

burlesque Egyptian. Enter COLETTE *dressed as a mummy and* MISSY *in a suit and solar topee as an archaeologist. They perform a pantomime during which the mummy awakes, divests itself of its bandages and, almost naked, seizes the archaeologist and executes a seductive dance which ends in a passionate kiss. They stay in a passionate embrace through a series of sounds, catcalls, shouts, jeers etc and one loud 'bravo, bravo' in* WILLY'S *voice. Eventually they break apart kissing their hands to each other. They stand quietly for a second or two.*

COLETTE   We've done it then. A public announcement.

MISSY   You can still get out of it you know. I've never made demands.

COLETTE   Oh Missy, you are sweet! You will come on tour with me sometimes, won't you? I have quite a lot of engagements, in spite of my bad notices.

MISSY   I'll be with you whenever you want.

COLETTE   Not all the time. It's so tedious and boring if you're not involved. But we'll meet. Rendezvous in exotic places – like Lyons station?

MISSY   Is it going to be all right, Colette? Is this what you want?

COLETTE   Absolutely certain, my love. This is me, on my own, without M. Willy in the wings.

MISSY   What about me in the wings?

COLETTE   That's different. (*Pause*) I'm going to write too you know. Publish under my own name. Just mine. Au revoir. See you in Strasbourg.
            They embrace and move apart to stage left and right.

MISSY   (*Staring straight ahead. Speaks as if composing a letter*) Dear Colette, longing to see you again. Eight months!

COLETTE   (*Similar posture, similar voice*) I can't wait. You can't imagine what an austere life I lead.

MISSY   Every moment apart from you is meaningless.

90

COLETTE   And now the tightrope walker's broken his leg and
            I have to double the length of my act. It's all
            rehearse, perform, sleep.
            *They turn and begin to move towards each other
            during the next little interchange, but still as if
            quoting letters.*
MISSY   Our meeting was so brief, so brief! And now
            another ten months.
COLETTE   The performing seals find the train journeys very
            difficult.
MISSY   When can you next come to Brittany?
COLETTE   My new dancing partner is divine. Don't worry, he
            spent half last night describing to me all the boys
            he had in the last ten years. What energy! I
            wouldn't have thought it possible.
MISSY   Why are your tours so long? It's inhuman. When
            will you come home?
COLETTE   I'm glad you liked my short stories. Not bad in
            three years – two novels and a play besides. I have
            a week off in Nice. Will you come down? My
            divorce has come through, by the way.
            *They embrace, separate and look at each other
            properly.*
MISSY   How well you look!
COLETTE   It's because I've decided that my music hall career
            is at an end. I feel so relieved. It wasn't fun any
            more.
MISSY   What will you do?
COLETTE   Write, naturally. Oh, I know I can't live off novels,
            but I can turn out articles. I'm going to be a
            journalist.
            They embrace and part.

SCENE 8. Parting

The BARONESS *and* LADY L *enter the acting area holding a newspaper. They search through it and they find the page they're looking for.*

BARONESS   Here we are. Oh, she's signed it. It's about time. All those anonymous articles were so coy.

LADY L   She couldn't keep the pretence up now her affair with Henry de Jouvenel is common knowledge. Do you think it will last?

BARONESS   Not for a minute. He's such a roué. (*Pause*) Do you think I could get to write articles for Le Matin too, if I were prepared to sleep with the editor? You see, my dear, you can turn to women for comfort and security but it's only the men who can help your career.

LADY L   Have you heard from Missy?

BARONESS   No. But they tell me she's claiming half Colette's possessions! In lieu of alimony I suppose.

LADY L   Poor Missy! Let's go down to Brittany to cheer her up.

BARONESS   Not me my dear, I'd find that house too sinister. Of course you wouldn't know, would you, that she's living there with the man she'd sorted out to be Colette's second husband!

             They leave the stage area. Enter COLETTE *and* MISSY *who stand facing each other awkwardly, each with baggage.* MISSY *is very dignified, very cold. The deep hurt, the almost unbearable loneliness must be clear.*

COLETTE   Don't forget to wear a vest, will you? Winter's almost here.

             MISSY *looks at her ironically whilst drawing on her gloves.*

COLETTE   I do care you know. (*Pause*) Please don't. We're not going to be those sorts of people who never speak to each other again are we? How can you wipe out so many years of friendship? (*Pause*) Missy?

MISSY	(*Slowly*) My dear, you have already wiped out thirteen years of marriage.
COLETTE	Oh, don't do that. Don't resort to meaningless comparisons, not you. It's unworthy.
MISSY	Indeed. I must remain the perfect gentleman to the end. The peasant's idea of the real true aristocrat, eh? Noblesse oblige and all that?
COLETTE	Yes! Because that's what you are.
MISSY	You have another aristocrat to admire now, I'm sure M. de Jouvenel has all the attractions you found in me and a few others which, alas, I can never have.
COLETTE	You know that . . .
MISSY	That you like women as well as men? Perhaps I'm not exactly a woman, though, am I? I've seen you, little sensualist, smile in delight at the lack of inhibition in the chorus girls' dressing room, feasting your secret greed on the forbidden fruits of the perfect breasts. But you haven't been unfaithful with a chorus girl, you've chosen a man. (COLETTE *turns away*) If you had to have a man, why couldn't you have Edouard? I was prepared for that. He was close to us both. I even prepared a double room for you.
COLETTE	And that was enough to put me off for life. I will not have my marriages arranged. (*More gently*) Edouard is a dear friend. I'm in love with Henry.
MISSY	Very well. I wish you every happiness. It's your life.
COLETTE	Don't talk as if this were the end.
MISSY	It is. M. de Jouvenel and I are hardly cut out to be friends.
COLETTE	Henry needs to be educated. In six months we'll all be having a giggle together at Maxime's.
MISSY	(*Angrily*) Don't play games Colette. You know the number of men, or women for that matter, who would be prepared to even acknowledge me in Maxime's can be counted on one hand. (*She holds*

93

out her hand) Adieu, madame.

COLETTE *slowly stretches out her own hand which* MISSY *takes and kisses with a cold bow and clicked heels. She picks up her suitcase and leaves.* COLETTE *stares after her on the point of tears.*

COLETTE (*Calling after her*) Don't bother to return all my things, you can keep them as a memento. (*Pause. The next bit is an afterthought said to herself*) Except my plants. I'll call round for those. You'd never know how to look after them.

She pulls her coat around her shoulders, picks up her case and walks away.

OLD COLETTE Who do I still feel so bad when I remember that goodbye? Why am I sad whenever I think about Missy? (*Long pause whilst she looks out of the window. She catches sight of a little boy in the park*) Oh the little devil! There he goes, his nurse after him. Just like Bertrand, those same sturdy little legs, that same defiance. (*Pause*) I couldn't tell Missy that part. Henry had two little boys, children, he had children and I wanted children. With two stepsons I was sure of a family. Little Bertrand, those wide eyes which could become so intense, so insistent. We were very close. (*Long pause*) Where is Pauline?

She picks up a small bell and rings it. Pause. Enter PAULINE *carrying a dish.*

PAULINE It's the fish you were ringing for I expect.

OLD COLETTE I thought it must have boiled away to glue by now.

PAULINE I started cleaning the stove and didn't want to interrupt. I had to wait for it to cool, anyhow. There wasn't any hurry, was there?

OLD COLETTE No. I'm sorry, I just had a funny moment, that's all. I expect I needed to speak to a person not an invisible animal. Put the dish in the middle of the floor so he'll have to come right out.

PAULINE If he condescends to notice it. Cats can be very

94

	stubborn. If you ask me, the best thing to do with that one is to send it back where it came from. I'll take the carrots. (*Sees that they are untouched*) Oh, I see.
OLD COLETTE	I'm afraid I didn't get around to them.
PAULINE	Hmm! There'd be hell to pay if I didn't get around to lunch.
OLD COLETTE	Pauline, your language has really degenerated over the last few years.
PAULINE	No harm in calling a spade a spade. I've realised that as I've got older.
OLD COLETTE	You were such a demure little thing when you first came to us.
PAULINE	I should think so! I daren't open my mouth except to the children. When you're hardly more than a child yourself and you go up to work at the big house, you daren't put a foot out of line.
OLD COLETTE	I was just thinking of those days, of Renaud and Bertrand. The games we had.
PAULINE	Aye, they were nice when they were little. All kids grow up, though.
OLD COLETTE	Yes.
PAULINE	There's too much made of babies if you ask me. Women are dying to have babies as if that's the end of it. As if they aren't starting something that goes on forever changing their lives. Perhaps they wouldn't be in such a hurry to do it if they knew how it would all turn out. Since you haven't done the carrots your meal might be a bit late. And I'm not having that fish on the floor for ever. If it's not gone in a couple of hours, it'll go to a more deserving cause. *Exits.*
OLD COLETTE	There, did you hear that? There's plenty of hungry moggies slinking around those dustbins. (*Sighs*) Sido would have had you out of there in two seconds. (*Pause*) Is Pauline right, would Sido not have had me if she'd known what I'd grow up

95

into? I believe she would.

SIDO *comes into the playing area. She is old and frail looking.*

SIDO   Minet-Chéri, I've told you not to worry me with your anxieties about my health – that is my problem. Let us get on to yours. You are making a terrible mistake if you are planning to marry this young man Henry. I liked the other better, the one you call the idiot. What marvellous things you could write with that idiot. You'll give everything that is most precious to that Henry and he'll only make you unhappy. Oh you'll survive. You survived the first, which is always the worst. Hold your head up Minet-Chéri. Look at me. What are you thinking? How well you look in pink. Remember, you are never to wear mourning for me, you look dreadful in black. And for goodness sake don't marry that man.

She walks away. MISSY *enters the stage area. She is softer, more defenceless than in the previous scene.*

MISSY   (*Looking at audience, as if quoting from a letter*) My dear Colette, I had resolved never to get in touch with you again, then I heard yesterday of Sido's death. I also heard that you wouldn't attend the funeral. I understand. You were right. I knew she was the best friend you'll ever have. You have lost your dearest friend, there are others still here. You have hurt me but I will never stop loving you. I wanted you to know that. Some time we shall meet. I shall never have a daughter. Perhaps you will. They tell me you're now pregnant. Clearly M. de Jouvenel is all a woman could wish for. Good luck. I truly mean it. Au revoir my friend.

Long pause. The telephone, which is near the divan, rings. OLD COLETTE *looks at it for a long time. Eventually she picks it up, with great reluctance.*

OLD COLETTE   Hello (*Her face changes to a radiant smile*) Hello,
Maurice. What a surprise. How are you my dear?
(*As she listens to the reply her smile broadens and
she begins to laugh*) Come now, Maurice that's too
much (*more laughter*). Oh no, really? (*Smiles,
nods*) Oh my darling, it's so good to hear you.

 END OF PART ONE

PART TWO

The fish has been cleared away, OLD COLETTE
*is sitting in her daybed looking out of the window,
humming a tune. Her eye is caught by something
on the window sill. She takes up her magnifying
glass, leans towards the object of her attention,
gives a quick gasp, leans back a little.*

OLD COLETTE   Oh no! My patient little friend! But why? Why
now? You weren't starving I know. I counted the
flies in your larder every day. (*She puts the glass
down*). I didn't know spiders could just die, just
like that, for no reason when they're fat and
healthy. People do that, of course, but of all God's
creatures humans are the most unreasonable. It's
very disappointing of you to go and turn up your
toes all of a sudden. I've lost too many old friends,
too many. I was relying on you.
Telephone rings, she picks up the receiver.
Hello (*Pause*) How's it going? (*Pause*) Oh la la!
Those horrible schedules. I hope you're remem-
bering to eat properly. (*Pause*) Do as I say, mother
knows best. (*Pause*) Bel-Gazou, say all that again.
(*Pause*) That's ridiculous child. How old is she?
(*Short pause*) Yes it matters, it matters. (*Short
pause*) How old does she look? Late thirties? But
think child, that's nearly as old as you are. No, No
and No! Older or younger perhaps. (*Pause*) Bel-
Gazou your father was at the front line during most
of the war (*Definitely*) and we still loved each
other. My God, it's twenty-five years since we

98

divorced; it's seventeen since he died, when is all this nonsense going to stop? I don't want to hear any more about it. It's impossible I tell you. (*Pause*) Bel-Gazou, no more! You mustn't listen to these jealous lies. They are so many they are ridiculous. If I believed everything I heard, your father would have spent every minute of every day making love to a different woman. No time for politics, no time for journalism. Come on, it's too much. He wasn't such an extraordinary lover believe me. Listen will you come to lunch on Sunday? (*Pause*) Do try, Maurice would be so pleased. (*Pause*) All right. And remember, you must learn to laugh at these people. See you soon. (*She replaces receiver, leans back, eyes closed*) Do we never stop paying for the mistakes we make in love?

SCENE 9. *Black Magic*

Enter COLETTE. *She is in a state of agitation. She is clutching to her a small photograph, in a frame. Places this very carefully on the table, then sits and stares at it fixedly. She gets up to open a drawer from which she produces a letter. Sits again, unfolds it and places it on the table by the photo. She stares at them both malevolently, her lips moving as if in silent incantation. From off stage* MARGUERITE'S voice *is heard.*

MARGUERITE Hello Colette, my love, are you there?
She enters almost immediately. COLETTE *starts guiltily, grips the letter, puts the photo face down. Seeing* MARGUERITE'S *questioning look, she puts the photo upright again, puts the letter back on the table.*

MARGUERITE What the devil are you up to?
COLETTE Not the devil, just a bit of magic.

99

MARGUERITE	Don't be flippant, I can't stand it when you try to joke, with your eyes so big and tragic. It's grotesque. Who is that woman?
COLETTE	(*Passes her the photo*) Don't you recognise her Marguerite?
MARGUERITE	(*After studying her for a few seconds*) Yes, I do now. It was the hairstyle. It must have been taken a few years ago, it's not much like her now.
COLETTE	It was the best I could get hold of. I had to involve myself in backstairs intrigues to get that.
MARGUERITE	Colette, really!
COLETTE	Really what?
MARGUERITE	You're being very silly.
COLETTE	For a change. Don't you think it's about time? I've had enough of being reasonable. Don't you think one gets more out of life when one is unreasonable. More fun? More consideration even? People handle you with care don't they? Instead of saying 'Colette will understand. She always does', they say 'Watch out, don't do that because Colette might blow up.' What are you laughing at?
MARGUERITE	Just listen to yourself! The inveterate analyst! I'm afraid you're stuck with your intelligence my dear! You might be silly sometimes, but you'll always be the clever little observer! What are you doing with this photo, truly?
COLETTE	Truly, casting a spell. Haven't you ever done it?
MARGUERITE	Well, I . . .
COLETTE	Most of my friends have. And someone is doing it to me now. I know she is. Why else do I keep losing things? Accidents don't usually happen to me, yet in the last three days, I've burnt my right hand, banged my head, fallen over in the Metro and cut my thumb. Stop laughing!
MARGUERITE	(*Suddenly serious*) No, I shouldn't laugh.
COLETTE	So I'm trying to give her a few nasty moments in return. Nothing drastic – migraines, stomach aches, perhaps even a broken ankle if I try hard.

MARGUERITE	(*Passes back the photo, which* COLETTE *replaces on the table*) Is that a letter from her? May I read it?
COLETTE	I'd rather you didn't. It's very vindictive. (*Pause*) She would like to kill me. (*Helplessly*) Oh well, there are people I would like to kill, sometimes. I understand how she feels, but I can't let her destroy me.
MARGUERITE	What pathetic fools we are! You and I always realise what's happening to us, we have no illusions, and we just watch it happen without lifting a finger to stop it.
COLETTE	I've just told you, I'm lifting my whole burnt hand with its lacerated thumb!
MARGUERITE	Come off it. It's Marguerite Moreno you're talking to. You're not going to tell me you really believe playing around with schoolgirl spells is going to make any difference to anything?
COLETTE	It might. (*Pause*) What can I do Marguerite? How can I keep Henry except by hurting my rivals? You would have thought I'd learned something from my years with Willy, wouldn't you? I didn't, I'm as helpless as ever. I love Henry passionately and we're worlds apart. He wants to hurt me, Willy didn't *want* to hurt me, he just did! Why, Marguerite, Why? I've never hurt him, I'm devoted to him. Is it the war? This dreadful separation. Me in Paris, Bel-Gazou in the country. If we could have lived more together as a family, it would have been all right. Perhaps it will be all right when it's all over.
MARGUERITE	(*Takes her hands*) Ma Colette. Look me in the eyes. Will it ever be all right? *Long Pause.*
COLETTE	No.
MARGUERITE	(*Still looking directly at her*) Don't pretend it's because of Henry's infidelity either. COLETTE *turns away.*

MARGUERITE	Ma Colette, my little independent one, you are about as devoted to Henry as your cat is to you. It isn't your nature to give yourself completely for ever. Completely for five minutes, an hour perhaps even, before your total attention is claimed by something else.
COLETTE	At least I'm faithful.
MARGUERITE	Don't make a virtue of it. With you it's an instinct. Deep down the only person you're being faithful to is yourself.
COLETTE	Don't you like me, Marguerite? After all these months we've spent together without our men, listening to the cannons, comforting each other, do I find you don't like me?
MARGUERITE	(*Laughing*) My dear I love you. We're two of a kind. Two actresses, always listening to ourselves, thinking we could have said that line better. *They leave.* OLD COLETTE *sits up, takes a pile of letters, sifts through them shaking her head. She puts them back, leans back.*
OLD COLETTE	(*To audience*) Could it be possible? God knows there were plenty of other women then, but I was sure all Henry's so-called children had already tried to stake their claims. Why wait until now? It doesn't sound as though this woman wanted to trade on it though. She simply told it to Bel-Gazou as a fact. Perhaps I should . . . Yes maybe I should. (*She picks up the receiver and begins to dial, thinks better of it, replaces receiver*) I'll write to her. No, I'll leave it alone unless she brings it up again. I'll only say the wrong thing. I always say the wrong thing.

SCENE 10. The Nanny

Enter COLETTE *and* NURSIE-DEAR

COLETTE	She seems to be a little peaky altogether. She's usually so bright.

NURSIE-DEAR	No, she's very well.
COLETTE	Nursie-Dear, I sometimes think the English idea of 'very well' is not quite ours. You are used to pale, thin people with long noses and woollen socks, that is normal for you. We French picture health rather differently.
NURSIE-DEAR	I would like to point out to madame that I am in a better position to say what is 'normal' for her daughter than she is. I see her every day, whereas madame only every few months.
COLETTE	I know, I know, I was only teasing.
NURSIE-DEAR	I'm sorry, I thought it was a criticism.
COLETTE	Good heavens, no. I chose an English nurse because everyone said that English nurses are the best and now I find out it's quite true. You're wonderful with her, she adores you. Of course there are times when you are much stricter than I would be, but she doesn't seem to hold it against you.
NURSIE-DEAR	She knows I do everything for her own good. She can rely on me to be quite fair. She trusts me. She knows I'll always be here whatever happens.
COLETTE	If she's not just a bit out of sorts why did she have such a tantrum?
NURSIE-DEAR	If I may speak plainly, I think madame was somewhat indiscreet, to say the least, as soon as she arrived, to announce her intention of going away so soon.
COLETTE	But it's best not to pretend. If I suddenly told her I was leaving it would be worse.
NURSIE-DEAR	The very best thing, madame, would be to continue to spend more time with us. That would be the very best thing of all. A child whose parents are separated, madame, should be able to rely on at least one of them!
	She exits.
COLETTE	(*Goes down stage centre, as if quoting a letter, to audience*) My dear little one, what a time you had

looking for mushrooms. They are so good when they're freshly gathered. And you find them in full summer too, not like chestnuts which are a mixed blessing, for they remind us that school term is about to begin. I have some good news for you. I am buying a house in Saint-Tropez, a funny box of a place with a terrace and a vine covered wall. There's a vineyard, a few fig trees, a few pines and, best of all, next to a beach. We'll spend next Easter there, you and me.

SCENE 11. Bel-Gazou

A girl sings offstage. Enter BEL-GAZOU. *She is fifteen. She hums to herself as she hitches up her skirt and makes as if dipping her toes into the water and paddling. She picks up a shell.*
COLETTE *watches* BEL-GAZOU *for a few seconds before joining in with her humming.* BEL-GAZOU *starts but doesn't turn round.*

BEL-GAZOU	Hallo, maman.
COLETTE	It's the first time I've heard you sing since we arrived. So you do like it here?

BEL-GAZOU *shrugs her shoulders.*

COLETTE   I think I'll wet my toes too. I'll wait until later to swim. (*Paddles in beside* BEL-GAZOU) It doesn't smell like the Channel. Do you remember the mornings after a storm when there were great palm trees of seaweed flung across the shingle? The hard salt smell, the wet shiny rubber smell as you walked over the rocks? (*Pause*) I'm sorry! Of course you do. You belonged there. But the Mediterranean will begin to tell its own stories. Give it time, eh? What a lovely shell you've found, let me look.
She takes the shell and examines it whilst BEL-GAZOU *walks away to sit on a rock.* COLETTE

104

	walks over to her, holding out the shell. BEL-GAZOU *takes it with a strained smile, looks away.*
COLETTE	I've brought you a picnic. I was at the market very early, so I had the pick of the fruit and cheese. You know there's a wonderful little baker, so I bought us two greengage tarts. You should have seen the fish! I'm going to make you a proper bouillabaise tonight. And, look (*She crosses back to hamper, takes out a bottle which she brandishes triumphantly*) we'll drowse ourselves into siesta-time with the local wine.
BEL-GAZOU	I'm not very hungry, maman (*Pause*) And wine always gives me a headache.
COLETTE	Oh!
BEL-GAZOU	I'm sorry.
	Pause, BEL-GAZOU *will not look at* COLETTE, *who looks fixedly at her.*
COLETTE	Bel-Gazou . . .
BEL-GAZOU	Don't, mother.
COLETTE	Has your father . . .?
BEL-GAZOU	The way I feel has nothing to do with him.
COLETTE	That can't be true.
BEL-GAZOU	It is true! I don't want to talk about him. I'm not going to spend the rest of my life listening to each of you telling me bad things about the other. You're two separate people now.
COLETTE	I have never told you 'bad things' about Henry, never. I don't want him to turn you against me, that's all.
BEL-GAZOU	I'm fifteen. I can make up my own mind.
COLETTE	All right.
BEL-GAZOUR	You think so? You think it's all right? Why don't you ask me what I've decided about you, maman, all on my own.
COLETTE	(*Her voice slightly shaky*) When a fifteen-year-old girl stands in judgement she is bound to be a little severe. Oh dear, how stern you look. A little bit pompous. Don't say my beautiful warbler is grown

	up into a solemn owl. Do you remember the owl in the attic at Castel-Novel, the one you all thought was a ghost?
BEL-GAZOU	Don't do that! You're always doing that. You must take me seriously now. It's not like it was, everything's changed.
COLETTE	Is it a young woman I have to deal with? Those English boarding schools! Are you sure you wouldn't like the tiniest bit of bread with a tomato? (*She digs in the basket and brings out a tomato*) Look at the size, Bel-Gazou and the colour! It was picked just after dawn, I expect. Don't you think it has a newly awakened look?
	BEL-GAZOU *runs over to her mother, snatches the tomato, throws it into the sea. She thumps her, sobbing in sudden rage.*
BEL-GAZOU	Stop it, stop it! I hate you!
	COLETTE *grasps* BEL-GAZOU's *wrists whilst the girl continues to struggle, sobbing. When she subsides* COLETTE *lets go.* BEL-GAZOU *moves away.*
COLETTE	I'm sorry.
BEL-GAZOU	So am I! I never wanted you to see me cry ever again.
	Pause.
COLETTE	(*Gently*) I really wanted this holiday to be a very precious time for both of us. You and me together in our new house, planting seeds.
BEL-GAZOU	Why do you have to pretend? It's not our house, it's your house. I shall hardly ever be here. Papa already has plans for where to take me for the next school holidays. So I'm not going to plant any seeds.
COLETTE	Bel-Gazou ...
BEL-GAZOU	You won't miss me any more than you will miss Renaud or Bertrand, and they aren't even your children. You'll miss me less than them because they're boys. All my friends say their mothers love

106

	their brothers better. You told me grandmother Sido loved Achille better than you.
COLETTE	I gave birth to you, your stepbrothers came to me from outside. Don't you see how much difference that makes?
BEL-GAZOU	No. It never made any difference at all.
COLETTE	My child, when I saw you, that little baby that had formed inside me and came out quite finished, I thought you were the most perfect thing I'd ever seen. When I look at you even now I can hardly believe that such beauty. . . .
BEL-GAZOU	That's just it, when you look at me you think about me, when I'm not there you forget me. Beautiful. You call your dogs and cats 'beautiful'. You even called that awful snake we had once in Paris beautiful. It's like what those English girls said!
COLETTE	What did they say?
BEL-GAZOU	They said you must be very wicked for two husbands to have stopped loving you. They said they supposed it was because you were a famous writer and women can't be proper wives and mothers as well as famous writers!

COLETTE *turns away from her daughter for the first time. She is struggling with tears which will not, however, fall.*

BEL-GAZOU	(*Very upset now, needing to get it all out!*) That was nothing, they said worse than that maman. There's another French girl at the school. She told them terrible, terrible lies. She crossed her heart that they were true. Everybody in Paris knew, she said.
COLETTE	What everybody in Paris knows is not worth knowing.
BEL-GAZOU	But maman, it's not true, is it? It couldn't be true that you and Bertrand, you and Bertrand . . . Bertrand is like a brother, my brother, maman! And you are so old! She said in the end that was why Papa left you, because he found you and Bertrand . . .

	She sobs hysterically. COLETTE *puts her arms around her, hugs her very tightly.*
COLETTE	Oh, Bel-Gazou, oh my little one, of course it's not true. That you should come to hear of such things.
BEL-GAZOU	What a wicked girl she is, isn't she maman?
COLETTE	Girls at school are often wicked.
BEL-GAZOU	I do love you so much.
COLETTE	I love you too, more than anything on earth.
BEL-GAZOU	(*Breaking away, calmer now*) She said, this girl, that it must be true because you'd written about an old woman and a young boy in love in your novel *Chéri*. But people don't write about themselves in their books do they, maman!
COLETTE	(*To audience*) Of course you don't! *They exit.*
OLD COLETTE	Of course they don't! But that's what they said about *Chéri* and my heroine. 'Colette has described herself,' they said. She must have, look how well she plays the part of Léa on stage, they said. Some said: she should leave that to proper actresses. But she doesn't want to, they said. Not this part. Not this elderly courtesan who is in love with a boy almost like her own son.

SCENE. 12 *Chéri*

	LEA *and* CHARLOTTE *come into stage centre.* LEA *is played by* COLETTE. *They embrace.*
CHARLOTTE	Léa, my dear! Where have you been all this time? And not a word. We were all so worried.
LEA	There was no need. You see how well I'm looking? I've had a wonderful holiday!
CHARLOTTE	I'm glad. But who with? That's what we've all been dying to know dear. Who with?
LEA	(*Giving her a playful tap*) And that's just what I'm not going to tell you.
CHARLOTTE	Oh don't be mean. You are in amazingly good

	form I must say. No-one would think you were pushing fifty.
LEA	Very few people are allowed to think it either, so don't shout so loudly. Your voice is indiscretion itself, Charlotte.
CHARLOTTE	So Chéri is always telling me. He's been furious with you by the way.
LEA	Oh, why?
CHARLOTTE	Don't ask me. Who understands one's children? What a relief to get that boy married.
LEA	The lovebirds have settled happily into their nest?
CHARLOTTE	So so. The usual arguments. You and I have been wonderfully lucky to be spared the life of the couple. Marriage can be terribly sordid.
LEA	Why were you so anxious to push Chéri into it then?
CHARLOTTE	What else could I do? Marie-Louise has a fortune, her daughter will always be comfortably off. What a heaven-sent opportunity! The girl's so pretty and she's in love with Chéri. You know Chéri needs to be kept in a manner to which he's been accustomed – in idleness and luxury. You need a doting wife for that. It's much more secure than a string of ageing mistresses. No offence meant, dear.
LEA	None taken, dear
CHARLOTTE	I did wonder whether you were sulking a little when you stayed away for so long.
LEA	Charlotte, really!
CHARLOTTE	(*Quickly*) Chéri's such an ungrateful little beast, I don't suppose he ever said thank you for all you've done for him.
LEA	(*Gently*) There was no need. I think, I'm sure I love him as unselfishly as any mother.
CHARLOTTE	I never took it for granted even if he did. You gave yourself to him unsparingly. Our bodies have been our fortune. We don't usually give them for free.
LEA	Perhaps we're reaching the age when it's our turn to pay.

CHARLOTTE	Heaven forbid! I can do without it, thank you very much.
LEA	Perhaps I can too, who knows?
CHARLOTTE	I've got better things to do with my money. Which reminds me, I wanted to talk to you about my latest investments.
LEA	If I'm not mistaken, here's your daughter-in-law.
CHARLOTTE	Why so it is! What's the matter with her? She looks as though she could do with a dose of salts. ESMEE *comes into the acting area. She is very tense.*
ESMEE	Good morning, belle-maman. Good morning Madame Léa. I hadn't realised you were back.
CHARLOTTE	Nobody did, my dove. She's becoming so sly. Are you all right child. You haven't got a little secret to tell us?
ESMEE	(*Laughs bitterly*) Hardly! (*Pause*) Chéri didn't come in last night. He wasn't back when I left. But then perhaps you already know that. Perhaps Madame Léa has given you the information.
CHARLOTTE	How would she know?
ESMEE	(*Tearfully*) Oh don't play games, please! (*To* LEA) Did he spend the night with you?
LEA	Yes, Esmee, he did.
CHARLOTTE	Oh really Léa! You should have spanked him and sent him home. It's too bad.
LEA	It's not that easy, Charlotte, you should know that.
ESMEE	Especially when you don't want to. When you like a young man for pleasure, as a relief from the rich old fools you tolerate for money.
CHARLOTTE	Don't be impertinent, Esmee. If your mother hadn't tolerated so many rich old fools you wouldn't enjoy the luxury of a marriage with a poor young man.
LEA	(*To* ESMEE) I'm sorry. It was none of my doing. I promise you it's the last time. It won't happen again.
CHARLOTTE	(*To* ESMEE) It takes a little while to get used to a

	different diet even if it's better for you. Chéri's bound to find cream cheese a little bland when he's used to old camembert.
LEA	Thank you. You always did have a gift for finding the right words.
CHARLOTTE	(*To* ESMEE) We have so many little tricks, Chéri's used to expert handling. I realise it's difficult but if you and Léa would get together and discuss things frankly, you could learn a lot from her. Aunty Léa was one of your favourites.
ESMEE	I'm sorry, belle-maman. I find this conversation disgusting. Good morning.
	ESMEE *leaves the playing area.*
CHARLOTTE	(*To* LEA) Wasn't that somewhat indiscreet?
LEA	I told you. I didn't want it to happen. It was my first night back. I was caught off guard. That's the end now Charlotte.
CHARLOTTE	I hope so. I didn't think you were one to cling on like that. There's no need after all. (*She looks critically at* LEA) The way you are now I'd say you've got three or four more years before you hang up your corsets.
LEA	(*Laughing*) Not as long as that believe me. I'll retire when I want to, not wait till I have to. Perhaps you'd better tell me about these investments.
CHARLOTTE	(*Takes her arm*) Well, if my sources are to be believed, you can double your capital in no time at all. I wouldn't risk it yet, I have to make a few more discreet enquiries, if you see what I mean, but I'm very excited. The Stock Market's better than sex any day.
	They exit. OLD COLETTE *fidgets for a moment or two, picks up the telephone receiver and dials.*
OLD COLETTE	Could I speak to Mademoiselle Colette de Jouvenel, please. (*Pause*) When should I call her then? (*Pause*) Not any time today? (*Pause*) No. Yes. Just say her mother phoned and says she's

111

very sorry. Nothing else. Thank you. (*She replaces the receiver*) As usual. I don't quite know what for, but I'm sure she'll expect me to be sorry. Perhaps I should try to see her on her own for a while when she comes round, without Maurice. Bless his heart, he's the best stepfather in the world. There isn't a day of my life goes by without my thanking God for Maurice. God and Marguerite.

SCENE 13. *Maurice*

Enter COLETTE *and* MARGUERITE. *They stand well apart on stage as if phoning each other from a long distance.*

COLETTE	You did, I know you did. It was all deliberately set up.
MARGUERITE	It was nothing of the kind. How could I do that? It was all pure accident.
COLETTE	It was a put-up job. It was at your dinner party I first met him. Then you engineered my stay with you to coincide with his visit. You're a wicked schemer.
MARGUERITE	You do like him darling don't you? He's admired your books for ever.
COLETTE	I like him. I like him very much indeed. (*Pause*) Marguerite he's only thirty-five.
MARGUERITE	So?
COLETTE	Well!
MARGUERITE	I've told you before, never admit to your age. You don't look 52.
COLETTE	I've invited him to lunch.
MARGUERITE	Splendid.
COLETTE	After all, your choice is probably better than mine would ever be.
MARGUERITE	How true, my love, how true.
	They put imaginary receivers down and exit.
OLD COLETTE	(*Picks up little bell rings it. She gives a deep sigh*)

112

	What a pity, I met the nicest man I've known when I could no longer bear him any children.
	Enter PAULINE *with a cup of hot chocolate.*
OLD COLETTE	Good heavens!
PAULINE	I was nearly at the top of the stairs when you rang. I thought you'd be needing this round about now.
OLD COLETTE	What an angel you are. (*Takes the chocolate*) Have you time to sit with me for a while?
PAULINE	I've time, have you? You haven't forgotten you've several appointments today. Maybe you should rest.
OLD COLETTE	Sit down please.
	PAULINE *sits.*
OLD COLETTE	The kitten is going to have to be put down. The vet rang.
PAULINE	(*Pats* OLD COLETTE's *hand sympathetically*) Such a tiny scrap of a thing.
OLD COLETTE	I'm glad I hadn't mentioned it to Maurice. I suppose I realised it from the beginning. You never like to admit there's no hope for such young things. (*Pause*) The spider's dead too, would you take it away? How's your arm?
PAULINE	A bit better since the weather got less damp.
OLD COLETTE	You don't take enough care of yourself. How often do I have to tell you? You think you're still young and sprightly. You must take things more gently.
PAULINE	Fat chance in this house. I'm trying to do out the kitchen. It looks a right mess. Mind you the oven looks a treat now. It's almost like new. I was up till midnight to get it finished.
OLD COLETTE	That's not a good idea. What would I do if you became ill?
PAULINE	I won't. By the way, whilst I was up to my elbows in greasy water, that M. Cocteau called. Just been to an opera. Wanted to tell you all about it. Such ridiculousness. I told him you'd be fast asleep at that time of night.
OLD COLETTE	Oh, poor Jean! He's always a delight at any time. Of course I wasn't asleep.

113

PAULINE	He should have more sense than to come round to people's houses after eleven.
OLD COLETTE	But that's early in Paris.
PAULINE	There's no reason why Paris should be different from anywhere else. I know how he goes on sometimes, chatter, chatter, chatter.
OLD COLETTE	(*Laughing*) You've never liked him.
PAULINE	No. Besides he had a friend with him. He could have been anybody come from anywhere.
OLD COLETTE	If he was a friend of Jean's . . .
PAULINE	Oh yes, I'm not that green. You know M. Cocteau and his like pick up 'friends' all over the place. I can guess how this one earns his living, it was written all over him.
OLD COLETTE	Was he pretty?
PAULINE	Pretty! Say what you like it's not natural for men to look like that. (*Pause*) They can't help the way they're born, I know, but they don't have to make it worse by making up their eyes, and wearing scent and (*With outrage*) lipstick!
COLETTE	Why shouldn't men wear make-up?
PAULINE	Because it makes them look like women, that's why.
OLD COLETTE	Our instincts must be weak if we're confused by a touch of powder or kohl! (*Pause*) I've heard it said that old women, like me, shouldn't wear make-up either, because it's grotesque to try to look like young women.
PAULINE	You need kohl for your bad eyes.
OLD COLETTE	And lipstick for dry lips, I suppose? There's nothing wrong with any of us enhancing the beauty God gave us. I wouldn't have opened a beauty salon if I hadn't believed that. It was a silly thing to do all the same, for a woman of sixty. Pauline, do you remember some of our customers? What a fiasco! Dreadful women! They just wanted to see me in the flesh. They had no intention of buying anything. And they all brought the books to sign.

	They probably never even read them. What a farce! I'm obviously not a business woman. (*Pause*) This chocolate's delicious. I used to leave a drop for that spider, you know, because Sido had a spider who liked hot chocolate. Came down from her bedroom ceiling at three o'clock every morning for its little treat! This one wasn't interested though, too many fat flies.
PAULINE	It's only country spiders who do things like that. Parisian spiders are far too grand.
OLD COLETTE	Don't you think it's getting chilly in here? Pass me a shawl will you? Put one on yourself.
PAULINE	Gracious no, I don't need a shawl.
OLD COLETTE	Well, I certainly do. I thought it was spring yesterday and now it's freezing in here again.
PAULINE	Of course it is. You have to expect it. Spring doesn't come all at once, just like that. We could still have snow, you know, even this late.
OLD COLETTE	Like on my last wedding day, 3rd April, 1935. It wasn't even cold that morning either, yet the flakes filled the sky like a burst eiderdown. I made Maurice stop the car so I could listen to the snow whispering amongst the dead leaves. Beautiful April snow balanced in tiny piles on the wild honeysuckle.
PAULINE	Aye. It's not as nice in the city.
OLD COLETTE	We should have a fire. With the spider and the kitten gone the only living animal I can call my own is the fire. I've learned how to look after it. Did you know, Pauline, that fires don't like even numbers? Three logs burn better than two, seven than four.
PAULINE	I'll be needing to order some more logs.
OLD COLETTE	It's a pity there are no apple logs to be had. They smell the best. Do you think you could find any?
PAULINE	(*Very firmly*) No.
OLD COLETTE	Make sure they're beech then.
PAULINE	It's not that easy.

OLD COLETTE	I don't suppose it is. Try though, try. It's not easy, but it's possible.
PAULINE	I suppose you expect me to send my man to the Bois de Boulogne with a saw, eh!
OLD COLETTE	(*Laughing*) You're as good a hand with a saw as he is. All those trees you and I and Bel-Gazou carved up between as at Curemonte during the war. What women can find they can do when their men aren't there to do it for them. You used to swing an axe in a most businesslike fashion.
PAULINE	You had to do everything for yourself when you were living in that ruin.
OLD COLETTE	I've never seen you enjoy yourself so much. I felt very guilty bringing you back to Paris, but that was where I was used to spending my wars.
PAULINE	God help us if we have to go through any more like the last.
OLD COLETTE	I certainly won't. It's not quite ten years since liberation. I should think Europe will manage another ten of relative peace.
PAULINE	(*Gets up*) I'll go and get some wood and paper,
COLETTE	Fetch out a bottle of burgundy will you? I'll have a glass with my dinner. Just one. You two can finish the bottle. Mind you, I want one of those goblets, not an apology for a glass!
PAULINE	(*As she goes*) We should none of us have to go through that again. Nobody should ever! *Exits.*
OLD COLETTE	(*Looks out of the window for a long time. Pause*) We always wonder afterwards how we managed it. We never think we could do it again. But we would.

SCENE 14. *The Brisk Young Woman*

COLETTE *and a* BRISK YOUNG WOMAN
enter. COLETTE *now walks with some difficulty.*

116

BRISK YOUNG WOMAN	I think at long last, madame, your patience and untiring efforts may be rewarded.
COLETTE	They'll let him go, mademoiselle?
BRISK YOUNG WOMAN	Not yet. They are prepared to give him special treatment. Would you like to sit down, madame?
COLETTE	No thank you.
BRISK YOUNG WOMAN	You are lucky to have friends in high places. Some of your colleagues are listened to with great sympathy by the German High Command.
COLETTE	Yes.
BRISK YOUNG WOMAN	My father is a university professor who has admired your work for a long time. He introduced me very early to your books, which I too enjoyed. I thought the Claudine series a bit er . . . how shall I say? Cheaply sensational? But then they were a collaboration were they not?
COLETTE	And collaboration is not a good thing, mademoiselle?
BRISK YOUNG WOMAN	In literature sometimes not. In life it is often essential madame, is it not? There is no point in fighting the inevitable. When you lose a war you have to make the best of it.
COLETTE	Mademoiselle, if you don't mind, perhaps you could give me further details . . .
BRISK YOUNG WOMAN	Of course! I don't want to preach to the converted. Your husband's safety is the most important consideration. It was really most unfortunate you married a Jew, wasn't it?
COLETTE	(*Dryly*) I wouldn't say so mademoiselle. It was my marriage with the French aristocracy that was my big mistake.
BRISK YOUNG WOMAN	Yes but under the circumstances. . .
COLETTE	Mademoiselle, please.
BRISK YOUNG WOMAN	Yes of course. As I said the commander has been asked to give your husband preferential treatment, good food, permanent employment in the camp and above all, his safety guaranteed.

COLETTE	And his freedom?
BRISK YOUNG WOMAN	Really madame, we must not ask for the impossible.
COLETTE	No. We shall just try to convert it to the possible – thank you mademoiselle, you are very kind. Perhaps under the new conditions we shall be allowed to communicate with each other?
BRISK YOUNG WOMAN	(*Laughing*) M. Goudeket will be too busy for letters.
COLETTE	Thank you. Good morning, mademoiselle.
BRISK YOUNG WOMAN	Just a moment madame. Concessions such as those I have described are not given lightly.
COLETTE	Ah!
BRISK YOUNG WOMAN	The occupying forces need all the help they can get to maintain the stability of the country.
COLETTE	What do you want from me?
BRISK YOUNG WOMAN	From you nothing at all. From your husband, not much, co-operation. (COLETTE *looks at* BRISK YOUNG WOMAN. *Pause*) Just to keep his ears open around the camp. Report back. Make a note of names. That sort of thing. You will be allowed to write and put this simple proposition to him.
COLETTE	(*Slowly*) I am to say 'My dear Maurice, I love you, I miss you. Please for my sake collaborate, inform, betray your fellow prisoners, your friends'.
BRISK YOUNG WOMAN	A woman of your literary sensibility could put it less starkly.
COLETTE	I refuse.
BRISK YOUNG WOMAN	I don't think you quite understand. The alternative is death. There is no other choice acceptance – or death.
COLETTE	Very well. I choose death.
BRISK YOUNG WOMAN	You choose death! For your husband!
COLETTE	*We* choose death. Good morning, mademoiselle. *The* BRISK YOUNG WOMAN *moves out of playing area.* COLETTE *moves downstage, faces audience.*

118

COLETTE	(*As if quoting from a letter*) 23rd December, 1941. Dear Marguerite, No more news of Maurice except what I was given over the telephone by someone who'd moved out. Morale is excellent. 36 in a room. Food less disgusting than we feared. Straw on the floor to sleep on. I just wait. That's the most difficult part. (*Pause*) 13th February, 1942. If I haven't written to you before, my Marguerite, it's because there's been a great weight inside me for the past eight weeks. Maurice, who's been 'away' since 12th December, has just been returned to me. In my heart of hearts, a tenacious, hopeful obstinacy always survived. There are two of us again sending you love and kisses. *She exits.*
OLD COLETTE	And then we waited together, like everybody else, until the day when it was all over and the soldiers would come back. What a sight rue Vivienne was then, every house blossoming with flags, badly dyed threadbare pieces of cloth. Everybody laughed and cried at the same time out in the street. And at night in the garden all the windows, dark for four years, opened their eyelids and the light poured out. And they were all singing the Marseillaise, all the windows, flung open, waved black hands against a golden backcloth. Voices breaking with love. (*Pause. She makes too sudden a movement, feels a stab of pain and gives a gasp. Slowly, cautiously, she leans back*) So, my old friends, my insidious aches and pains, you think we're going to be all alone together do you? Nothing else to speak to, nothing else to listen to but you? You won't get it all your own way. I still have more allies than you think. As long as there's a sparrow hopping about on the balcony, I'll have company. There are other sounds louder than creaking muscles and grinding joints – a fly fanning its wings, dead leaves dancing. (*Closes her*

eyes) Even in this room I can smell the change in the soil as winter ends – seeping through the cracks. I can hear chrysalises turning over, restless. (*Opens her eyes, a look of great happiness*) And I have my ghosts, my dear, dear ghosts, especially the one who is always there at three in the morning to share with me that ecstasy you feel before dawn. *Enter* SIDO.

SIDO (*To audience, as if quoting a letter*) Yes, Minet-Chéri, I lied to you for the sake of a quiet life. I sleep here alone. Leave me be all of you, you and your brothers. Don't come telling me stories about burglars and such like. Give me a dog if you want, that would be all right, but don't make me have someone else in the house with me all night. I just can't bear anyone sleeping in my house now who isn't one of my own flesh and blood. It's undignified. I'd rather die. It's more proper at my age. By the way, you know when I had my operation I had two white flannel nightdresses, well, I've cut them up and made a new one to be buried in. It has a kind of a hood with the most beautiful lace round it and round the sleeves and collar. I hate cheap cotton lace. I am furious because Victor Considerant gave my sister Caro a magnificent ebony coffin with silver handles, which he had made for his own wife, who, when it came to it, was so swollen she wouldn't fit in. That stupid Caro was so taken aback she gave it to her cleaner. Why didn't she give it to me? It would have suited me so well. Don't let this letter worry you. It's all right I'm just trying to sort things out, so that when the time comes I shall go quietly and respectably, out of sense of decency. (*She turns to* OLD COLETTE*)* Don't bother about death Minet-Chéri. It's nothing – how you die is important.

OLD COLETTE I know, maman, I know.

SIDO In my garden, everything died at the end of

120

	autumn. Without that there could have been no Spring. No room for the new shoots. You remember?
OLD COLETTE	I remember.
	COLETTE *takes her hand. They smile at each other. They freeze. The rest of the company come forward. The following speech is divided between them.*
FIRST ACTRESS	On 3rd April, 1954 at about 8.20 in the evening Sidonie-Gabrielle-Colette died in her bed overlooking the summer gardens of the Palais Royal.
SECOND ACTRESS	The family's request for a burial service at the Eglise Sainte-Roche was refused by the Archbishop of Paris.
THIRD ACTRESS	Colette, was, however, given a State funeral, a unique honour for woman.
FOURTH ACTRESS	Of her death, her husband Maurice said: 'She seemed intensely happy. She began to speak very carefully, but not to any of us. As far as I could guess it was to Sido she spoke'. She had returned to her starting point.

BLACKOUT.

BONDINGS

A play for voices

Characters in order of appearance

LOU   *Psychoanalyst. Andreas Salomé; student of Nietzsche & confidante of Freud. Lover of Rilke.*

FRIEDA   *Lou's patient.*

RAINER   *Rilke, poet and lover of Lou.*

GENERAL   *Lou's Father.*

FREUD

SCENE 1

Spring 1922. LOU'S *consulting room in Göttingen. The window is open. Birdsong. Rustling of branches in a gentle breeze. A cuckoo.*

LOU (*Reading the end of a letter*) And so, my dear Anna, you see how vivid are the memories of my stay with you. Every detail of those weeks remains. When all is quiet in the evenings I imagine myself back walking with your father, sharing so many ideas. Please come to see me soon. You will love this house. There are forests behind us and foxes in the garden. We have chosen to settle amongst animals and trees. Tell your father I will write soon. A long letter. I am already half way through. Your dear friend, Lou.

Pause. She folds the paper, puts it in an envelope. A distant clock strikes.

Five minutes to clear my mind. I would so like to talk to Sigmund. Letters take so long. I need his opinion.

Sound of a front door bell somewhere else in the house.

A few minutes early! She's always been late.

Steps approaching room. A knock on the door.

Come in!

Door opens and closes.

FRIEDA Am I early?

LOU Not much.

FRIEDA I thought I would be. I hurried, I ran. I was angry. I'm sorry.

LOU It doesn't matter.

Pause.

FRIEDA I'd like to sit and get my breath before I lie down. I

125

wanted to get here. I had to get here, but I'm not
quite ready. Are you? Of course you are. You are
always ready. So serene. Ready for anything
(*Pause*) You don't answer? Of course not. It's not
in the contract. (*She takes a deep, nervous breath*) I
nearly didn't come. But what else could I do?
That's what I'd planned. I have to, don't I, or we'll
get nowhere. I have to come even if I really want
to go down to the river instead and throw myself
in. No, I didn't want that. I never want that. I never
want to end it.

LOU   Will you lie down now?
FRIEDA   Lie down and look away from you. You are
                nobody after all Frau Andreas. A presence behind
                me, so that I don't feel like a madwoman when I
                talk aloud. All right. (*Pause*) Sometimes I wish I
                were your friend and not your patient. Then I could
                look into your eyes.
                Pause.
LOU   (*Inside her head*) She has the most beautiful eyes.
                Violet, like Rainer's. An artist's eyes. She sees, she
                really sees. I wouldn't ever want her to look at me
                for too long.
                Pause.
FRIEDA   I am in a very bad mood. I don't think I should
                come to you when I am in this state. I will probably
                be spiteful, tell you all sorts of lies. I've tried to tell
                the truth so far. Or have I? Would you know if I
                told you lies, invented for myself a heroine who
                never was, could never be? Would you?
LOU   Perhaps. Perhaps not.
FRIEDA   Would it matter?
LOU   No.
FRIEDA   I thought not. Anyway we don't want that, do we?
                We want a shocking truth. My husband is waiting
                for the dreadful revelation which will release my
                frozen fingers and let me paint again.
LOU   You don't want to paint again?

126

FRIEDA	Of course I do.
	Pause.
LOU	(*Inside her head*) Do you? Your hand is yours, obeying you, no-one else. It is your voice which is saying, 'Be still'.
FRIEDA	Of course I want to paint. I have an exhibition organised for the end of the year. I have to do so much. I haven't nearly enough work. And what I have is useless. (*Pause*) It was looking at my paintings made angry. I was up at dawn, trying to find something of merit, disgusted with it all. What I *could* do is marvellous. I can imagine whole canvasses as they will be, with every brushstroke. For the first time in my life I can see the pictures sharply before they're painted, and I can't pick up a brush! (Pause*)* My husband came in when I was about to take a knife to that rubbish with my good hand. My patient Heinrich! 'Don't', he said. 'They're beautiful. You'll break my heart.'
LOU	(*Inside her head*) A knife. Andreas carried a knife. He turned it on himself the night before our wedding.
FRIEDA	I frightened him, Frau Andreas. I have always frightened him. That's why he loves me. He loves being afraid. I'm like a wild animal he wants never to tame. I turned towards him, the knife held high. He was petrified. I could have pierced his heart, or my own guts, he was powerless. (*Pause*) He is a good man. He cares for me like a baby.
	Fade out.

Late that night. LOU *is writing. Owls in the garden. A distant dog.*

LOU (*As she writes*) She is so mercurial, (*Pause*) excitable. I would welcome your views. (*Pause. She puts down the pen*) I can't write any more tonight. Nothing I write quite describes what I mean. (*Pause*) I feel very weary. She tires me. It's odd she uses me up as Rainer used to use me up sometimes. She is demanding too much, she is only a patient. To him I gave everything, gladly. My Rainer, my monstrous, genius boy.
Sound of waterfall, getting louder as we hear a breathless RAINER *climbing up to it.*

RAINER (*Panting*) Lou, oh Lou it's magnificent! Oh come on, Lou.

LOU (*Panting, and speaking slowly as she climbs up*) It's all very well for you, child. I prefer to take my time. Take my hand, help me up, if you want me to arrive more quickly. There, that's better.

RAINER I would like to hold your hand in all the most exciting moments of my life. You make everything complete. Look, isn't it wonderful?

LOU It is truly magnificent.
Pause.

RAINER Come away, over here behind these rocks where it is less noisy. I want to talk. Come on. Here. You sit here and I'll put my head on your knee. I like looking up at you. Your red hair is like a halo. Madonna! Virgin Mother. (*Pause*) Lou, I know your body, I feel so at one with it that it is me. We are truly one flesh.

LOU That is what love is.

RAINER But it is a very particular love. It is something I remembered from before I was a separate being. I am joined to you by a cord Lou, that's why our bodies are so familiar, we are one blood. If they put out my eyes, I would see you; if they cut off my

128

LOU	limbs, destroyed my senses, I would still carry you in my blood. You are my mother, my wife, myself. You are my brother. We are all the richer for being two alike and different. I am the woman in you, you the man in me. We are both sister and brother to each other from an age where incest was holy. We are closer than husband and wife. *Pause.*
RAINER	Lou, I'm jealous of your husband.
LOU	(*Laughs*) My silly boy!
RAINER	I know you have never slept with him.
LOU	Nor ever will. I told you. We were destined to be man and wife. We shall remain together until death. But without physical union.
RAINER	How can he bear it?
LOU	He only tried once to take what was forbidden. When I was asleep. I awoke to find myself strangling him. (*Emphatically*) I will not give myself to him. He is a soul brother. *Pause.*
RAINER	You gave yourself to me.
LOU	You are a blood brother. It was right. It was easy.
RAINER	Stroke my hair. And my eyelids. I love your touch on my face. When your hands move over me I feel like Adam being moulded by God into a living being. Whatever I become you have created. (*Pause*) Does Andreas like me?
LOU	I haven't asked him.
RAINER	Isn't he jealous?
LOU	He's never said so. I started to tell him about our times together; he said he didn't want to know. Is that jealousy?
RAINER	No! Oh no.
LOU	I'm not the right person to ask. It's an emotion I've never experienced.
RAINER	Of course not. You could only be jealous if I loved someone else. And I will never, never, never do that. *Fade out.*

SCENE 3

LOU'S *consulting room. It is windy and rainy. The window panes rattle and the rain beats, heavily at times, on the window.*

FRIEDA   I was the one who did the wooing. I'd met him at a party. It was partly his looks, mainly his courtesy. All the stuff about solidity, security, it was all there. Kind, intelligent, rich, handsome – he was most eligibile. Serious-minded with it. A true connoisseur of the arts. I made sure I was around wherever he was around. He liked me, no more or less than he liked several of my friends. At last I invited him to my studio. He was overwhelmed. It was a time when I was inspired. Big, bold compositions. He looked at the paintings, then he said, 'You don't paint like a woman!' And he fell in love.

LOU   (*In her head*) She radiates power, energy, strength. Yet there is still more blocked inside her. She is filled with an enormous force too great for her body to release. Is that genius? I would so like to see her paintings. I shall ask her to bring in some drawings.

FRIEDA   You'd heard of my family before I came here?

LOU   No.

FRIEDA   You don't belong to our set. I wouldn't have been able to see you if you did. (*Pause*) You're Russian, so I suppose you aren't really up with who is who here. You're an outsider. We've been here for generations. Where were you born?

LOU   That doesn't matter.

FRIEDA   Of course it matters where you were born!

LOU   It doesn't matter to you and me.

FRIEDA   You don't have a Russian accent.

LOU   Please, Frau von Wendel. You must concentrate on yourself.

FRIEDA   I sometimes find myself very boring. Please call

	me Frieda. If you must be formal, call me by my professional name, von Tramm.
	Distant clock strikes. Pause.
	That's it, isn't it? End of session.
LOU	Yes.
FRIEDA	I would like to think that one day, you and I will sit and talk for as long as we want. Then you will tell me where you were born. (*Pause*) I could find out. Perhaps I will.
LOU	(*Firmly*) Please don't. Your case will not progress if you divide your attention between me and you. Thinking about me is simply a relief from thinking about yourself.
FRIEDA	I don't like thinking about myself.
LOU	That is very clear. Good morning Fräulein von Tramm.
FRIEDA	Good morning.
	She leaves. Door opens and closes. Steps across hallway. Outer door opening and closing. Pause.
LOU	(*Deep sigh*) This will take a long time. I think I'd like to listen to some music. Russian music.
	She picks up a record, places it on the gramophone. Something not too intense.
	I'm always called 'The Russian Woman'. Strange, in St Petersburg I was called German. Perhaps I was really more French. Why should it matter? It didn't matter to the Tsar. He loved Papa. But then everyone loved Papa.
	Fade music right down. Bring in sound of sleigh bells and horses hooves. Street noises.
LOU	(*Little girl voice*) Papa, are we really going to the fair?
GENERAL	Yes my sweet.
LOU	It's warm under your fur coat. It's very, very cold today. (*Pause*) What will we see at the fair?
GENERAL	Jugglers, rope-dancers, monkeys doing tricks like men, a woman with a snake round her neck, a dancing bear.

LOU	You're nice. And big and warm. (*She kisses him*) I love you very, very much. (*Pause*) I wish we didn't have to go home.
GENERAL	We're not going home, we're going to the fair.
LOU	Afterwards. I wish we didn't have to go home afterwards. I wish we could go away and live in a house in the woods and sleep under your fur coat and listen to the wolves.
GENERAL	All alone?
LOU	Just you and me. Can I marry you when I grow up?
GENERAL	I'm afraid not.
LOU	Let's go away and live in the woods, Papa?
GENERAL	Without Robert and Alexander and Eugeny? Don't you want Eugeny to come too?
LOU	No. He can visit.
GENERAL	And Mama?
LOU	No. I don't want her to come.
GENERAL	I have to go to work.
LOU	I'll cook your dinner for when you come home.
GENERAL	You'd be lonely.
LOU	No! I *am* lonely now; I wouldn't be lonely with you.
	Fade out sleigh bells and street noises. Music fades back up.
LOU	Strange, how you can be lonely with so many people around you.

LOU   (*Reading a letter*) I think that you must be very
        careful. From everything you tell me, this woman
        is becoming too important. There are patients who
        make most fascinating case studies, who rightly
        take up our thoughts and energies because they
        allow us to advance our science. I foresee a desire
        to intervene in some way. She must not become
        personally important. Besides, so far you have
        learnt very little. Most of what she says, if you
        have told me everything, hardly goes deeper than
        the exchange of confidences between women
        friends over tea. Are you well? Be careful. You are
        more delicate than you believe. I have had a heavy
        cold which I can't shake off. I need a rest.
        Pause. No longer reading.
        Perhaps I should have stayed in bed today. I can
        scarcely find the strength to move about the house.
        Perhaps later I'll feel better. Perhaps the dream
        will have faded. Horrible. Three nights in a row!
        Perhaps I should tell Andreas? (*She laughs*) No,
        not Andreas.

SCENE 5

LOU'S *consulting room.*

FRIEDA   I felt so happy. It was a happy, happy dream. It was the colours made me ecstatic, I stood at the edge of the yard, watching each truck arrive laden with fruit, piled high with ripe fruit. Strawberries first, then raspberries and loganberries, blackcurrants, redcurrants, gooseberries, bright green, and then, oranges, lemons, peaches and apricots. And fruits I didn't recognise. Strange shapes, subtle shades of pink and yellow. Truck after truck emptied into the yard in mounds. Men came out of the factory with shovels and piled them into wheelbarrows. They were all dark-skinned with soft brown eyes, and they wore blue and white uniforms. I followed one inside. He emptied his barrow into an enormous cauldron of simmering blood-red stew. Attached to the cauldron was a string of copper pipes, all of them polished until they were brilliant. Out of the last one poured a stream into rows of winking jars which passed by one at a time. And a mechanical arm put a lid on each one. (*Pause*) What does it mean?

LOU   What do you think it means?

FRIEDA   I don't know. I thought you would explain it.

LOU   No. You must explain it.
Pause.

FRIEDA   Well after all. It's simple.

LOU   Is it?

FRIEDA   I want to paint again, that's all. In my dream it was the same thing.

LOU   As what?

FRIEDA   As painting.

LOU   What is painting?

FRIEDA   What do you mean?
Pause.

LOU   What is painting? (*Pause*) For you.

134

FRIEDA	Thank you for the prompt. I suspect you shouldn't have given it to me?
	LOU *is silent.*
FRIEDA	I don't know how to answer that. It's a silly question. You want me to talk about something which has nothing to do with words. Nothing, nothing. I'm tired of words, of questions. 'Talk to me about it, tell me about it' Head stuff! My painting isn't from the head! (*Pause*) It comes from somewhere deep and dark and terrible. (*Pause*) All those classes – still lives, naked bodies like statues. 'Paint what you see, Fräulein von Tramm. Don't you see the way the back bends, the breast curves?' I saw, I saw, and I *felt*. The fruit, the flowers, the dead animals, the living thigh came into me through my skin not my eyes. (*Pause*) They entered my body through all my pores and the only living art was through my hand.
	Long pause. A dog howls in the distance.
FRIEDA	(*Slowly*) Now there is no way out at all. They are still crowding in. I cover myself from head to foot, I close my eyes, block up my ears. It's no use. My hand hangs like a bloated toad. It's too much. (*Sharply*) It is too much! too big, too big!
	FRIEDA'S *voice fades down as* RAINER'S *voice fades up overlapping each other for a moment echoing on the* 'TOO BIG!'.
RAINER	(*A voice of utter panic*) Too big! You are the big thing that is too close. You come too close! No! I don't want it! I don't, I don't! The big hard thing coming close, closer, into me, becoming me! You are too big. You are taking my blood. I hate you, I hate you!
LOU	Hush, Rainer, it's all right.
RAINER	No, no, it's not all right.
LOU	You're safe with me. I won't hurt you. Let me hold you.
RAINER	No! I don't want to be touched! I feel raw, opened

	up all over.
LOU	(*Gently*) Give me your hand. Just your fingers. See how soft my fingers feel on yours? There. It doesn't hurt. And if I stroke your face, if I kiss your eyelids, very gently, my lips can soothe you. You are *whole* Rainer, I make you whole. I don't take from you. There, you see? Look at me! Touch my hair. There.
RAINER	I love you!

LOU   (*Reading a letter*) Your Fräulein von Tramm
             sounds most interesting. I do think you are in
             danger of confusing the issue, whatever you say.
             Her voice fades into FREUD'S *voice.*

FREUD   She is a particular, a unique case. Yes, we can
             make comparisons. Yes we even make general-
             isations. How else can we build our science? There
             must be clear-headed observations – your head, it
             seems, is a little less clear than usual. Detail, you
             need much more detail if you are to proceed
             effectively. It does no good to keep harking back to
             resemblances with Rilke. You are always trying to
             tie things together. You have a synthetic approach.
             A womanly approach. Tidying up to make things
             comfortable. There is too much ambivalence. It is
             too messy. Your hysteric is more than a little para-
             noid. Keep your distance.
             Pause.

LOU   Don't I always keep my distance? Womanly? Am I
             unmanly? Tidying, harmonising, reconciling, seeing
             the whole, making the whole, yes, that is womanly.
             (*Pause*) Is that all? Children? Don't women bear
             children? Should I have borne a child? Should I
             have let another person grow inside my body?
             Whose child? Who could have taken me? Who
             would I allow to take me? I gave to Rainer. I opened
             myself up and gave what I wanted to give. He was
             the child I made to give me pleasure. I made him
             outside my body. I made him, I took him a lover/son
             I cared for him, he became my poet, my great,
             beloved poet. Until I lost him and he lost himself.

FREUD'S VOICE (*In her head*) I like what you say about art and
             artists although it is not entirely my view, as you
             know. A bridge between the sayable and unsayable
             – a good way of describing what is after all a kind
             of neurotic symptom! As you so rightly point out

both ends of the bridge must be there. If art loses touch with reality, there is catastrophe!

RAINER'S VOICE Lou, please tell me what is happening to me. Help me! I am going to hell. My body is dragging me down, my spirit is powerless. I am sliding, sinking into the unfathomable.

LOU There is no unfathomable! There is only the primal ground of your childhood. Go back, let yourself go back into forbidden memories. Your only help is there. Face them, face yourself! Look at yourself as Narcissus looked in the forest pool. With love for yourself and nature. The body isn't hell, Rainer, let your devils become angels.

SCENE 7

LOU'S *study. A knock on the door.*

LOU   Come in.

Door opens and closes.

LOU   Good morning, Fräulein von Tramm.

FRIEDA   Good morning, Frau Andreas. (*Pause*) Won't you call me Frieda?

LOU   I prefer the formality.

FRIEDA   I'm a lot better today.

LOU   Oh?

FRIEDA   My hand's still paralysed of course, but I feel positively cheerful. We're having a big party tonight for my husband's birthday. I would have invited you, if I thought you would have come. You wouldn't?

LOU   No.

FRIEDA   It's a pity there'll be people you'd find fascinating. Some of my art school friends. And people from the theatre. I have the most beautiful dress. I shall dance all night. (*Pause*) Are you interested in clothes, Frau Andreas?

LOU   No. (*Pause*) You know I'm not. Why do you ask?

FRIEDA   (*Laughs*) To annoy you! Of course I know you're not. Everybody knows you're not. It's an awful shame. You could look terribly attractive even at your age.

LOU   We should talk about your childhood.

FRIEDA   (*Quickly*) What a bore!

LOU   Why?

FRIEDA   I wanted to tell you about the party.

LOU   Did you have birthday parties when you were a little girl?

FRIEDA   Doesn't everyone?

LOU   Tell me about one.

FRIEDA   Which?

LOU   Any.

FRIEDA   One was much like another.

LOU	Was it? Which is the first you can remember? *Long pause.*
FRIEDA	They're all mixed up.
LOU	Think.
FRIEDA	It wasn't interesting.
LOU	Please Frieda. We'll get nowhere if you don't cooperate. Think. *Pause.*
FRIEDA	I was five. It was awful. I remember it because it was awful. (*Pause*) Most of them were very dull. Not like now. My parties are never dull now.
LOU	Why was it awful?
FRIEDA	Everyone seemed so cross. Not with me, I don't think. Just cross. The atmosphere was wrong from the start. Friends I didn't choose invited to tea. Little girls from good families. No little boys. I said no little boys. I didn't want my brother there. (*Pause*) I think, I don't know, it had something to do with him that they were cross. He and his friends played outside the nursery window and shouted and banged and were silly until my mother made them go away. (*Pause*) Those awful little girls giggled at the stupid things my brother kept shouting.
LOU	What stupid things?
FRIEDA	I can't remember. Just stupid, silly things boys say.
LOU	How old was your brother?
FRIEDA	A year older than me. A year and two months. I don't want to talk about him. He's boring. (*Pause*) It was his fault the party was so awful. He always spoilt everything for me. The little girls wanted to go out to play with the boys. They said they didn't. They said they were dirty and rude, but I could see they did. They started to pinch each other and made each other cry and I got very angry and shouted and threw a jelly on the floor and was sent to bed. (*Pause*) There, so what do you make of that, eh?

140

LOU	What do *you* make of it?
FRIEDA	Absolutely nothing. (*Pause*) Sorry. I'm not supposed to say that. I'll try. (*Pause*) I still feel the anger. I can see the red jelly on the white carpet. Anger first, triumph – red jelly on a white carpet. (*Pause. Low voice*) I hated my brother.
LOU	Do you hate him now?
FRIEDA	Now? (*She laughs*) No not now. He's nothing now. (*Pause*) He died last year.

SCENE 8

LOU	(*Reading letter*) My dear Anna, I'm so glad you had such a relaxing holiday. You need it. You work so hard. Perhaps I'll come and stay for a few days in a month or so. Andreas is away now, so the house is very quiet – no students, no all-night discussions about the origins of strange languages. I want you to meet him, he is a such a special man. So fine, so clever and yet so natural. He is brother and father to me and so much more. What is between us has always been immensely mysterious. I think you would understand. (*Pause. Voice inside her head*) Would you? No-one really understands. We hardly see each other, we are involved in different worlds, how can any-one know we were meant for each other until death? We don't even talk! *She remembers.*
RAINER'S VOICE	You don't even talk?
LOU	Not much.
RAINER	Why won't you leave him?
LOU	Never, never. I never want to – I can't. He is my husband.
RAINER	I could be your husband.
LOU	(*Laughing*) Oh no.
RAINER	Lou, he isn't a husband. You know he isn't. You live like brother and sister.
LOU	He isn't my lover, he is my husband.
RAINER	You make up your own meanings for words. Husband means sharing a bed! 'Wife' means allowing her 'husband' the freedom of her body.
LOU	(*Sharply*) No! It isn't to do with body. It is greater than that.
RAINER	You and I make beautiful love which is the most mysterious thing in the universe. Nothing can be greater than that, for me, nothing. I *am* your husband Lou, he isn't. Andreas is your protector

	that's all. He's a father. You think I'm a child but you are more of a child than I am. You can't leave your father. You want to run off and play with the naughty boys and come back for Daddy's forgiveness. Andreas isn't normal. He couldn't bear it if he were. He couldn't see us together. He couldn't have come to Russia with us.
LOU	He knows I will never leave him
RAINER	How does he know?
LOU	Because years ago when he was going to shoot himself because he thought I was going to be unfaithful I swore that I would die too. He was to shoot me first.
RAINER	You would have let him kill you?
LOU	My life is his, my body is my own.
RAINER	What if I say I'll kill myself if you won't leave him?
LOU	Silly boy! You're not going to kill yourself, you're going to become a great poet!

Back in present.

LOU	And so he is! The elegies are magnificent. The eighth is the unsayable poem of my most secret heart. The inexpressible is expressed. I must write to tell him, I must try to say all he says to me. This magnificence which is born of him is born of us. I have given him a child! At last my child has a child. Both my children, one flesh born of spirit, the other spirit of flesh! These stanzas are me, my home, the gardens of my childhood, my secret home, eternal paradise. Rainer, my beloved, I shall be grateful to you for as long as I live. Life's veritable consummation.

Fade up LOU'S *young voice. Robin's song.*

LOU	(*Sings*) A la claire fontaine
	M'en allant promener
	J'ai trouvé l'eau si belle
	Que je m'y suis baignée
	Il y a longtemps que je t'aime

143

Jamais je ne t'oublierai.

Sous les feuilles d'un . . .

GENERAL'S *voice joins in and finishes line.*

. . . d'un chêne

je m'y suis fait sécher.

LOU   (*Startled*) Papa!

GENERAL   I've been looking a long time for you, my pigeon.
All your guests have arrived. And you haven't
even got your party dress on. Mama is furious.

LOU   I like it here best.(*Pause*) I didn't want a party.
Listen to the robin.

GENERAL   It's too cold to stay out. Inside all the fires are
blazing away, it's like midsummer.

LOU   No, it's never like summer inside. Summer is only
in the garden.

GENERAL   Not now. There isn't a flower in sight. And the
pond is nearly frozen solid.

LOU   Isn't it beautiful? Let's go down to the river and
skate.

GENERAL   My dear, today you are thirteen years old. You
have guests, you have obligations. And you have a
new dress to show off and a present from me to
wear with it.

LOU   A present?

GENERAL   Weren't you wondering where my present was?
You didn't think your Papa hadn't bought you anything for your birthday? You shall have it when
you're dressed. (*Pause*) It is a special gift for a
beautiful young woman.

LOU   Papa, I don't want things to change. I want everything to be as it is. I don't want to be any different,
for people to think I'm different.

GENERAL   I don't know what you mean.

LOU   You do! When you call me 'a beautiful young
woman' you aren't talking about the little Lou you
used to carry on your shoulders.

GENERAL   (*Laughing*) Well we all have to grow up. (*Pause*)
And grow old. Listen Kätzchen . .

144

LOU	I'll only listen if you put your cloak round me and hold me close like you used to.
GENERAL	I'll do that if you walk back with me like a good girl.
	Pause.
LOU	All right.
GENERAL	Come on then, little squirrel. There.
	Sounds of footsteps on icy twigs.
	Lou, watching you grow into a lovely young woman is the greatest pleasure of my old age. It is a wonder and delight. Don't wish it away from me.
LOU	But you aren't the same with me. I am losing you.
GENERAL	Well, I will lose you before long. Some young man will steal your heart. Until then, put on your pretty dress for me, let me be the one to give you jewels.
	Footsteps stop. He gasps as LOU *throws her arms around and hugs him tightly.*
GENERAL	Hey, not so tight. I can't breathe! How strong you're becoming!
LOU	I will love you forever. No, don't pull away! Let's stay here holding each other. I can hear your heart beating Papa, I feel so much at home.
	Loud birdsong for two seconds. Fades down.
LOU	(*Voice of present*) I would have liked Papa to meet Rainer. To meet the child of my virginity. To know after all, I was faithful to him. If only he could have seen his child blossom as I have seen mine. How would he have moulded me, I wonder, if he had lived beyond my fifteenth year? What would I have become? What I am, what I have always been, alone in an enchanted garden!
	Music.

SCENE 9

LOU'S *consulting room.*

FRIEDA   It was such a relief to laugh. To be able to joke about my hand did me so much good. After the champagne I didn't care how coarse the jokes were. And for people to touch it, to hold it, kiss it, so it was no longer an alien repulsive thing.

LOU   Can you move it at all now?

FRIEDA   No but it doesn't matter as much. (*Pause*) We talked about you. About psychoanalysis. You'd be surprised how many people were strongly against it.

LOU   What do *you* think about it?

FRIEDA   If I weren't prepared to give it a go, I wouldn't be here, would I? (*Pause*) Several of my friends thought it was positively bad for an artist. That is destroyed creativity.

LOU   I have often found the opposite.

FRIEDA   Really? Tell me about it?

LOU   (*Annoyed*) Fräulein von Tramm, doubtless several of your friends also thought you were wasting your money. I'm beginning to be of that opinion myself. You know what the procedure is if we are to get anywhere at all. It doesn't include me telling you stories about my other patients. I think perhaps we should not see each other any more. (*Voice in her head*) Now she's turned round to look at me with those searching eyes. Horrified, she looks horrified. Well I won't be the one to turn away.

FRIEDA   (*Timidly*) You look very stern. (*Pause*) I don't want to stop.

LOU   Then please cooperate. Otherwise you are wasting my time as well as your money.

FRIEDA   (*Still tentatively*) That seems a bit . . . cold. People say you're cold – I didn't believe it.

LOU   The relationship between us is purely professional.

FRIEDA   Even professional relationships have warmth.

146

	They can become friendships. I feel warmth, even
	love, for the subjects of some of my portraits.
LOU	Outside this consulting room there is no relation-
	ship between you and me.
	Pause.
FRIEDA	Look, perhaps I should come more often. You're
	right, I haven't been taking it seriously enough.
LOU	You haven't been taking yourself seriously
	enough.
FRIEDA	I find myself boring. (*Pause*) You know I thought I
	wanted to look at you whilst I was talking, now I
	don't think I do. I'd rather lie down again. Yes,
	that's better after all. (*Pause*) You see, I feel
	instinctively that you can make things all right.
	Being with you is important. What I really want is
	for you to tell me about myself. I want you to look
	into my head without me having to say a word, and
	say 'This is what you are, Frieda. This is what's
	wrong. Do this and this and it will all come right'.
LOU	I'm not a faith healer, I'm a doctor.
FRIEDA	You're not a doctor. You're a writer, a novelist, a
	playwright, a poet. There's nothing scientific about
	you. Sorry, that's not an insult, it's a compliment.
	You aren't Doctor Freud. You have an artist's
	vision.
LOU	(*Very coldly*) Fräulein von Tramm, for the last
	time, you are not here to discuss me, Doctor Freud,
	or psychoanalytic method. What did you feel when
	your brother died?
FRIEDA	(*Startled*) What?
LOU	(*Precisely*) What did you feel when your brother
	died?
FRIEDA	Why do you ask me that?
LOU	Do your best to give an honest answer.
	Long pause.
FRIEDA	Nothing. (*Pause*) I hadn't seen him for some years.
	He'd gone away. To America. He was an
	American. He had become rich. Very rich. His

147

	wealth was vulgar.
LOU	How did he make his money?
FRIEDA	Some kind of business. I had very little contact with him. (*Pause*) He died in a car crash, in case you were wondering. He seems to have moved in a very fast set, from what we heard.
LOU	Did he have children?
FRIEDA	No. He wasn't married. (*Pause*) I hadn't seen him for eleven years. We never wrote much. We sent each other birthday greetings. (*Pause*) I was glad when he left. Cleared out of my life.
LOU	Why?
FRIEDA	(*Slowly*) He had always stood between me and the light.
LOU	What is your first memory of him?
FRIEDA	(*Hesitantly*) I'm not sure. I've put him out of my mind for so long.
LOU	Until his death?
FRIEDA	Yes.
LOU	You thought a lot about him after his death?
FRIEDA	Not a lot. Sometimes. Things came back. I had dreams. Sometimes.
LOU	Tell me.
FRIEDA	I can't remember. They were – disturbing. Nightmares, some of them. Nonsense. I can't remember. I just remember waking up feeling awful.
LOU	How awful? Frightened? Depressed? Angry? *Long pause.*
FRIEDA	(*Very low voice*) Guilty, I felt guilty.

SCENE 10

Later that night. Owl hooting. Clock strikes one in another room. Sound of LOU *moaning as if trying to speak. Eventually one word is spoken clearly and loudly.*

LOU Alexander! (*Voice of her thoughts*) Alexander. It was Alexander. That shapeless awful mound in the mud. My brother Alexander! I thought it was Father. Night after night the shape in the woods. I was sure it must be Father lying there under his big coat like a broken animal. Alexander. The face suddenly turned. Not dead. Not old, as he was when he died. Young. That beautiful young face looking into my cradle. That radiant boy! Alexander – arms around me! Alexander's smile when he led me out to dance, 'I'm so proud of you, Lou' (*Pause*) Why, oh why do I wake up terrified? *Fade up* FREUD'S *voice.*

FREUD It does sound as though you are beginning to make progress. Perhaps you have reached a real turning point. At the moment I am almost on the point of despair with a young man who is proving most extraordinarily resistant. I shall probably give up. We can't achieve miracles. The will must be there on the part of the patient. I had my doubts from the beginning. He was talked into the whole thing by his girl friend. I suspect she's the one who should be on the couch. From my one meeting with her I would say she has extraordinarily obsessive tendencies. I shall be most interested if you do manage to cure your young painter. By the way, what you told me about your brother Robert was dreadful. To come home from burying his son in the Crimea to find his house taken over by the peasants. To have to live side by side as one of them is unthinkable! But of course, since 1917, Russia has been characterised by the unthinkable.

149

SCENE 11

LOU'S *consulting room. Fade up* FRIEDA'S *voice.*

FRIEDA   I told you I frighten him. I like frightening him.
Maybe after all that's what really attracted me.
Subconsciously, that's the right word, isn't it?

LOU   Perhaps.

FRIEDA   He likes being frightened so I suppose we work
together well. It's what you'd call a good marriage.
(*Pause*) I don't want children. (*Pause*) All secrets
are safe with you, isn't that so? (*Pause*) He can't.
He's sterile. Not impotent, of course. (*Pause*) He
says he's happy for us to make pictures instead. He
looks after me so I can work. Poor Heinrich! He's
convinced he's married a genius. (*Pause*) I had a
dream last night. I wrote it down as soon as I woke
up. Aren't you pleased with me? I *am* cooperating
you see. (*Pause*) We were moving house, Heinrich
and I. To a castle. Big stone rooms, grand stair-
cases. I was alone, early in the morning. Heinrich
wasn't there – physically – but it was as if he were
present. He was me and I was him. We were both
there in me. I was waiting for the furniture. There
was nothing but an old chair by the window. At the
end of the great hall was a little doorway, with a
very old wooden door. I opened the door. It led into
cloisters, half ruined. In the middle was a pond. By
the pond stood a figure in a monk's robe. The
figure bent over the pond, then I woke up.
Pause.

LOU   Where does this come from?

FRIEDA   The castle from a book I was looking at yesterday.
Waiting for furniture? A friend of mine was telling
me earlier this week how long she had to wait for
her removal men to arrive.

LOU   The old chair?

FRIEDA	My grandfather's. He used to sit by the fire and sleep in it.
LOU	The little door?
FRIEDA	I don't know.
LOU	The ruined cloisters?
FRIEDA	The book again, I think.
LOU	The figure in the monk's robe, the pond?
FRIEDA	Just imagination I suppose. You'd expect to see a monk in cloisters. (*Pause*) You don't think that's a good enough explanation?
LOU	It's not an explanation at all. We haven't even begun to scratch the surface.
FRIEDA	Five out of ten?
LOU	I don't give marks.
FRIEDA	Just a little joke. Our sessions could do with lightening up, don't you think?
LOU	I think you should reflect long and hard on the shadowy figure. We'll talk about it next time. We've already overrun by ten minutes.
FRIEDA	May I come tomorrow? I'd like to see you four times a week if possible. *Pause.*
LOU	It would have to be very early.
FRIEDA	That's all right. How early?
LOU	Seven-thirty.
FRIEDA	Oh. (*Pause*) All right.
LOU	If you came always at the same time it might be a good thing.
FRIEDA	Good God! Four days at 7.30. Four days getting up at 6.30? (*Pause*) Why not, it might be interesting.
LOU	Tomorrow morning then.
FRIEDA	Yes. *Sound of* FRIEDA *sitting up. Tinkling bracelets. Rustle of silk. She sighs.*
FRIEDA	I'll try to have some complicated, colourful, fantastic dreams tonight then.
LOU	We rarely dream what we want.
FRIEDA	I know, that was another joke! I shall begin to think

	you have no sense of humour at all Frau Andreas.
	Good morning.
LOU	Good morning.
	Sound of door opening and closing.
LOU	(*In her head*) Why did I suggest that? Do I really want to begin the day with her? I like looking at her. Her face is extraordinary. So expressive. It says so much more than her words. It is more truthful than her words. She can't realise that. When she looks in a mirror she sees only the face she composes for herself. I suppose it's really the eyes. I can't see her eyes when she can't see mine. There is pain, such pain. (*Pause*) Something in me responds to that, not as a doctor, as a human being, a fellow creature. I want to put my hand on her shoulder, stroke her hair. There is such urgent need. So thin and taut and vibrant. She reminds me of . . . I don't know, I don't know. Is it Rainer? Is it really Rainer? Or is it someone else?
	Music fades down.

SCENE 12

LOU *is dreaming. There is a moaning wind throughout, not violent but disturbing and persistent.*

LOU   (*Frightened*) Father! Father! Where are you? It's so dark! I can't see you.

FREUD   Over here. Come over here.

LOU   It's so dark. No moon, no stars.

FREUD   Here. Take my hand.

LOU   Sigmund!

FREUD   Here little Lyola. Let me put my arm round you.

LOU   Papa?

FREUD   Let's sit here for a while. Sit on my knee. I'll keep you warm.

LOU   Papa, you have claws like a bear!

FREUD   No, only fur to wrap around you.

LOU   Sigmund. I don't understand. What are those lights in the bushes?

FREUD   The eyes of wolves come from the forests. See, now the clouds have gone from the moon, you can see them.

LOU   There's someone, a person bends them, looking at us. It's Rainer?

FREUD   No. It's your brother Alexander.

LOU   It's Rainer. There's someone else. Under the trees. Who is it? I can't see a face under the hood.

FREUD   Don't you know?

LOU   (*Calls*) Rainer! Rainer.

FREUD   He doesn't recognise the name.

LOU   He's going towards the figure. It's a woman. He's opening the cloak. Lifting the skirt. Rainer!

FREUD   He can't hear. Be quiet and give your father a kiss.

LOU   No! They are bears! Father they've turned into bears! No, no.

The last 'no' is a scream which wakes her up. The wind is still moaning outside her bedroom window. A gust rattles the shutters.

LOU	I must get up. Close the shutters. I wish Andreas were here.
	A wind grows in force, rushes through the trees like the sound of the sea.
LOU	It's only three o'clock. I've only been asleep for an hour. And now I feel wide awake.
	A dog growls outside the bedroom door. Starts to bark.
LOU	Bruno, be quiet.
	Dog barks more frantically. LOU *opens bedroom door.*
LOU	Bruno, stop it. It's all right! It's only the wind.
	The dog quietens to a growl.
LOU	Hush. It's only the wind. (*Pause, calls loudly*) Is there anybody there? See Bruno, look no-one!
	Dog rushes downstairs. Goes to front door, barks.
LOU	I'm sure there's no-one in the garden. Go on then, out if you must.
	Dog runs out barking. Comes back. Whines and whimpers.
LOU	Silly dog. It's just the wind, I told you!
	Distant sound of iron gate closing.
LOU	(*Uncertainly*) It's just the wind.
	Wind fades down.

SCENE 13

LOU'S *consulting room. The next morning.*

FRIEDA I didn't dream last night. Because I didn't sleep. I hate the wind. I adore thunder and lightning, but I can't bear the wind.

LOU You weren't . . . you didn't by any chance come up here, did you?

FRIEDA Up here? When?

LOU Last night. Late last night?

FRIEDA Why on earth would I come up here at night?

LOU I don't know. Did you?

FRIEDA Of course not! What an extraordinary idea.

LOU (*To herself*) She's lying. Her body tells me she's lying.

FRIEDA What put that idea into your head?

LOU The dog was disturbed. I thought I heard the gate closing.

FRIEDA What if you did? Why should you think it was me?

LOU You're right. It was an extraordinary idea. Please forget all about it.

FRIEDA I'm not in the habit of creeping like a thief at night. Surely there were a hundred other people you might have thought of first. And why should it be someone you know? Why not an intruder frightened by the dog? That's the most logical thought isn't it?

LOU Yes. I'm sorry. Please sit down.

FRIEDA And you are logical, aren't you? I wouldn't want to think that my doctor was given to irrational fantasies. About her patients!

LOU Please Fräulein von Tramm.

FRIEDA Oh for goodness sake! If you're going to have fantasies about me you may as well call me Frieda, once and for all. I always think of you as Lou. In my fantasies about you. Don't you think the relationship has gone well beyond the 'Frau' and 'Fräulein' stage?
Pause.

155

FRIEDA	Please, Lou. I'd feel so much better, so much easier. It's been one of the things holding me back. I need you to be Lou. I can't take naturally to Frau Andreas. She is someone else. *Pause.*
LOU	All right.
FRIEDA	Lou. Louise. I just want to say, first of all, before we start properly, that, when I couldn't sleep, I read. I read your latest novel. *Siblings.*
LOU	Frieda . . .
FRIEDA	(*Quickly*) It is extraordinary. That's all I'm going to say. Amazing. I couldn't call you Frau Andreas after spending the night immersed in your complicated sexual relationships.
LOU	Frieda . . .
FRIEDA	It's fiction, don't tell me. Nothing to do with the author. (*Pause*) I promise I'll say no more. I'll lie down and be good. (*Laughs*) Now I've read that book, I could tell you anything.
LOU	(*Voice in her head*) She *was* here last night. I'm sure of it. Why? She is different today. Softer. More vulnerable. Some of the pain has gone.
FRIEDA	I'm going to talk about my father. I thought you'd like that.
LOU	It's what you'd like that is important.
FRIEDA	Well then, *I'd* like that. My father is a very interesting man. (*Pause*) A powerful man. Handsome. I adore him. He has always given me everything I wanted. I was in love with him, of course, until I met my husband.
LOU	Why 'of course'?
FRIEDA	We all are, aren't we? All of us little girls? Surely that is one of the bases of psychoanalysis?
LOU	(*In the head*) She is beginning to make me angry.
FRIEDA	Just as little boys are in love with their mothers? I mean, we are all familiar with Dr Freud's ideas.
LOU	(*Suddenly, firmly*) Who looked after you and your brother?

FRIEDA	What?
LOU	Who looked after you and your brother? When you were small?
FRIEDA	We had a nursemaid. Later a governess.
LOU	Tell me about the nurse. Was she old?
FRIEDA	No. (*Pause*) She must have been very young I suppose when she came to us. I don't remember ever thinking she was old. She was younger than my mother. Younger than my wet nurse, who wasn't very old in spite of having two children of her own. Rosalie is her name.
LOU	The nursemaid?
FRIEDA	The wet nurse. She nursed both me and my brother because her two children were almost the same age as we were. I still see her. She's a lovely lady.
LOU	And your nursemaid?
FRIEDA	She was called Ilse. I don't see her any more. She left very suddenly. We never heard of her again. (*Pause*) She stayed with us until I was five. Then we had a governess. (*Pause*) I can see every detail of her face if I close my eyes. She had red hair, blue eyes, pale freckled skin. I've put her into many pictures. Always young. I don't want to imagine her old. She was very kind. She was always laughing, singing. She was from a village somewhere not far away. A second-cousin or something of Rosalie. She didn't quite know how to behave in a big city house. There were other servants to teach her. But she was a loving soul, that's what mattered. She slept in our room. When I had bad dreams I would creep into her bed. She would put her arms round me until I felt better.
LOU	And your brother? Did he creep into her bed too?
	Pause.
FRIEDA	(*Slowly*) I think he spent more nights in her bed that in his own. Now I think about it, God knows what they were up to. There was a lot of giggling.
LOU	Why did she leave, do you know?

157

FRIEDA	She was pregnant. What do you expect? She was pretty, charming, innocent. It's a wonder she lasted as long as she did.
LOU	Whose child was it?
FRIEDA	Who knows? My parents found out the evening before my birthday. She stayed for the party, then left. It was the first time I'd seen her cry. (*Pause*) It was my brother. He told them, I'm sure he did. I know he did. He said he didn't but he did. (*Pause*) He said he didn't know anything about it until the cook told us. Mother just said she had to go back to her family because of illness. Stefan knew, he must have done. He was always talking about getting babies. He wouldn't admit it even when I tried to make him confess.
LOU	How did you do that?
FRIEDA	I was a bit stronger. He was smaller that I was. He'd been a very delicate child. I could frighten him. I had a little knife I'd stolen from the kitchen which I kept hidden from him and threatened him with when I wanted to show him who was boss.
LOU	You were the boss?
FRIEDA	Yes. In a way. But girls are never the boss, are they? He was the son, the first-born. Nothing could change that. He was clever, he was pretty too. He talked well. He charmed everyone. My mother adored him. My father despised him. (*Pause*) Perhaps he saw in me all the qualities he wanted in a son. (*Pause. Suddenly, violently*) I wasn't in love with my brother! I hated him! I know you're trying to get me to say I loved him, but I didn't, I didn't!
LOU	I'm not trying to get you to say anything.
FRIEDA	Yes, you are. I've read your book. You make everything confused. You twist emotions. He loved me, yes, he did. But I never loved him. I never let him do anything. He was weak, he was like a little girl. (*Her voice begins to tremble*) His hair was fine like a girl's. My mother let him wear

158

it long. Father made him cut it. I cried, I liked to brush it, he liked me to brush it. It was cut very, very short. He hid in his room. He was weak. (*She begins to cry*) He was soft, a baby, a puppy. He loved me like a puppy. (*She begins to sob. Suddenly furious*) I don't want to talk about him! Why did you make me. I don't want to. You make me! He made me! I didn't want to! (*Very violently*) I didn't want to!

Pause.

FRIEDA   I'm sorry. I'd better go. I'll see you in a couple of days.

Music. Dramatic. Fading down.

SCENE 14

	LOU'S *dream. The same night. A howling wind.*
FREUD	And so you see, gentlemen, that we must not be surprised, or shocked by such desires, which are digressions, perversions of normal libidinal impulses.
	Pause. Wind moans.
LOU	Papa, there's no-one here.
FREUD	Of course there is. See those eyes in the dark. Shining in the dark.
LOU	They are wolves.
FREUD	They are my students.
	A long howl.
LOU	Andreas! That is Andreas! Where is he?
FREUD	I sent him down the mountain to fetch my handkerchief. I had the sneezes.
LOU	I must find him!
FREUD	He is perfectly all right. He will simply have stopped to buy some jelly on the way back. (*Pause*) Now, gentlemen, I would like to present to you the curious case history of the Sugar Plum man. We are fortunate to have the patient in question with us. Please come forward, Herr X. This is Herr X, gentlemen, who will be known to history as The Sugar Plum Man.
LOU	Rainer! Rainer, what are you doing here! Papa, that is not Herr X. It is Rainer.
FREUD	Herr X, you are willing to tell these gentlemen yourself about your curious obsessions?
RAINER	Yes, Doctor Freud, I am.
LOU	Rainer, no! Oh, no. Papa let me speak to him.
FREUD	Silence! The patient is very sensitive and must not be upset.
RAINER	I have found for several months now that in order to sleep I have to arrange half a pound, exactly half a pound of sugar plums, around my pillows, in a certain order.

160

LOU	Rainer!
FREUD	I must insist on silence!
LOU	I have to speak to him!
	Wolf howls. Much nearer.
RAINER	Frau Andreas, here is your husband, come to take you to the party.
LOU	Alexander is taking me to the party. My brother is taking me. And he is going to pin up my hair.
	Dance music. Early 1920s.
LOU	(*Breathless*) I must sit down. I can't dance any more.
FRIEDA	You dance beautifully, Frau Andreas.
LOU	I think this dress is not quite right for such an arena.
FRIEDA	But it is! It's beautiful. And you look beautiful wearing it. It suits your eyes. And your hair. Your hair is so fine and soft, like your dress. Shall we dance again?
LOU	Shouldn't you dance with your husband?
FRIEDA	Oh no! My husband can't dance. He's too young. He's only a baby, you know. I've left him in his cot.
LOU	Can I see him?
FRIEDA	Yes, of course. Come through here, into the nursery. Be very quiet so you don't wake him.
	Music fades to background as they enter another room.
LOU	How sweet he is! (*Pause*) Mama, can he be *my* baby?
FRIEDA	Yes my darling, Lyola, he is your baby.
LOU	Can I love him like you love me?
FRIEDA	Yes, my dearest.
LOU	But you don't love me.
FRIEDA	I do. I've always loved you. You silly girl. Come here, let me hug you. There.
LOU	Can I pick him up?
FRIEDA	If you're careful.
LOU	(*Crooning*) Come on little baby come to mama.

Come on. What's his name mama? What's my baby called?

Sound of puppy barking sharply!

LOU Oh! It's biting me! Oh!

Sound of crash and breaking china. Silence.

LOU (*Sudden heartbroken wailing*) Mama! Mama! (*Sobbing*) I've . . . broken . . . . my . . . baby!

She moans in her sleep. Clock strikes two. She wakes up.

LOU (*Breathing heavily*) I must get up. Read a little. (*Pause*) The nights are so long! All filled with nightmares. What's the matter with me? If only, if only her hand would get better. Where's Bruno? Bruno! (*More loudly*) Bruno! Where is he? He's usually here! Bruno! (*She gets out of bed opens bedroom door*) Bruno! Here, boy! (*She goes downstairs to front door. Opens it*) Bruno!

A yelp in the distance. Scampering in the undergrowth. Whining close by.

Bad dog! Where have you been? How did you get out? You should stay by me when your master's away. How did he get out? (*Pause*) The consulting room window! How could I have left it open? I never leave it open! Oh, Bruno, stay close by me. We aren't safe any more!

162

SCENE 15

	LOU'S *consulting room.*
FRIEDA	Before we start I've brought some pictures to show you. I could only carry small ones but I tried to pick out some of my best. I'm better working on a bigger scale. My most exciting work is much more abstract. Here, this is a portrait I did several years ago. It works, I think, although pastels are not usually my medium.
LOU	Who is it?
FRIEDA	A friend.
LOU	She's very striking.
FRIEDA	She is part Indian.
LOU	You're very close to her.
FRIEDA	Not at all. I brought these for you to see my work, not for you to probe my relationships. (*Pause*) I just want you to know me as an artist, not a silly, sick female. Perhaps you don't appreciate the mastery of technique involved.
LOU	Perhaps not.
FRIEDA	Pastels can be very sweet, sentimental. This is bold, as she's bold. (*Pause*) Do you like it? *Pause.*
LOU	It disturbs me.
FRIEDA	Good. Very good. What about the charcoal drawing? My grandfather's house.
LOU	Why is it so black?
FRIEDA	I saw it black that day. (*Pause*) And this?
LOU	(*Involuntary disgust*) What is that?
FRIEDA	(*Laughing*) A nightmare. Dramatic, isn't it?
LOU	(*In a low voice*) It's horrible. That . . . thing. That shapeless thing on the ground. It nearly fills the paper. It's human yet not human. (*Pause*) Please put it away.
FRIEDA	No! You haven't really looked at it. You haven't looked at it at all. Behind the shape there's a figure. Look! And there in the tree, a face. See?

163

LOU	Please put it away.
FRIEDA	It's a mixture of ink and charcoal with a light wash. I wanted the half-dark half-light atmosphere, where you can see without recognising. See the lines there and there? They balance the dark patches in the corner.
LOU	(*Violently*) Put it away!
	Pause followed by sound of FRIEDA *putting work away.*
FRIEDA	(*Coldly*) I can see you know very little about visual art. I'm sorry to have wasted my time. It is impossible for you to appreciate me as a painter.
LOU	(*Shaken*) I'm sorry.
FRIEDA	Don't mention it. Would you help me fasten my folder please? It's difficult with one hand. Thank you. After all, your job is to deal with the hysteric. So we'd better get on with it.
LOU	Frieda, I . . .
FRIEDA	(*Briskly*) I'm going to talk to you about my mother.
	Pause whilst she puts folder down and settles on couch.
FRIEDA	I don't want you to think my mother didn't give us all the love we needed, just because we had nurses and governesses. She did. She was a lovely, warm person, always gentle, always calm. She was a wonderful hostess – gracious, elegant. My father was very proud of her. We all were.
	Pause.
LOU	Go on.
FRIEDA	That's it. (*Pause*) Well, it's not much is it? She was very young when she married my father, scarcely over twenty when she became a mother. She wasn't strong, we had to be careful with her. (*Pause*) She was an only child of elderly parents. She was clever. She could have done many things. She married my father. I didn't blame her, she was a good catch. (*Pause*) I adored her.
LOU	How long ago did she die?

164

FRIEDA	Die? She isn't dead. Why should you think so?
LOU	You talk about her in the past.
FRIEDA	I thought you wanted me to be a child, to remember what I felt as a child.
LOU	And now. How do you feel now?
FRIEDA	How do I feel at this very moment? A bit angry as a matter of fact.
LOU	I didn't mean that. I meant how do you feel about your mother. Never mind. Tell me why you're angry now.
FRIEDA	You're not helping me. You don't, you *won't* realise me. I don't know what you want to hear. You don't seem to listen. Everybody said you were a good listener.
LOU	Everybody?
FRIEDA	Yes, everybody, everybody I spoke to about you. You're famous for listening. 'She's wonderful' they said. 'Her listening gives you strength.' Well, you don't give me anything.
LOU	(*Voice in her head*) Is she right? Am I resisting her this time? Am I shutting her out? Am I?
FRIEDA	Every time I've been to see you I feel worse. You're not a person. I need you to be a person. You're not there, you're a blank, you're a fraud. You haven't fooled me. This silence behind me is absence.
	Rustle of clothes as she gets off the couch.
FRIEDA	If I could move my hand I would draw you now, with your cool face. Not so cold though now I can look at you. Don't look away. Are you frightened to look at me?
LOU	(*In her head*) Yes, oh yes. (*Aloud*) No.
FRIEDA	Then don't drop your eyes like a schoolgirl. Forget for a moment what we're supposed to be doing.
LOU	(*Interrupting*) What you're paying me for.
FRIEDA	(*Angry*) Stop that! I will not be just another customer. I can't be. It won't work. God knows what you will have to be to give me the confidence

	to give myself up. I don't want to lie down and talk, talk, talk into space. Lou . . .
LOU	Please let go of my hand.
FRIEDA	Lou, I was expecting a baby. My husband's.
LOU	You said . . .
FRIEDA	I know what I said. It isn't true. Not quite. This time we had conceived a child between us. It was true that I didn't want children. I thought I was safe. It was some sort of minor miracle for him, for me it was a shock. I was unprepared. I had an abortion. Just before my brother's accident. (*Pause. Her voice trembles*) The day before. I killed my baby and my brother died. Tell me you forgive me, Lou!

166

SCENE 16

	Later that night. LOU'S *sitting room.*
LOU	(*Reads*) Dear Sigmund, I hope you are rested. This letter should be waiting for you on your return to say, 'Welcome home'. I am determined that I too shall take a holiday soon. When Andreas returns I shall take a long trip, maybe to Paris. I need to be amongst light and life and music and crowds. There are several of my friends who would be only too glad to accompany me. I have decided to finish with one of my patients, the painter with the paralysed hand. We have come to a halt. I am convinced that I am not the right person for her. As you know, there are one or two of our colleagues who would do as well or better than I. I have been re-reading Rainer's Elegies. They are so exquisitely beautiful, and I see much of our experience of Russia in them, but I wish that he were not so alien to his body. (*Stops reading. Normal voice*) I must write to Rainer too soon. I'll write to him soon. Now, it's impossible. When I even think of it, I feel more naked than when we made love. I can give him no comfort. I can give him nothing. I feel quite impotent. I feel as though I've failed him. I've never failed him. Never! *Fade down on last word.*
RAINER	Make me a child, Lou.
LOU	You are a child, my baby child. I have made you.
RAINER	Make one for me, with me.
LOU	No! Our love isn't about that.
RAINER	Make a man from me whose flesh will be whole-some. My child from your flesh will be clean and strong.
LOU	No. I can't. I won't. That isn't my destiny.
RAINER	The child of our passion.
LOU	No.
RAINER	Then may God damn this vile matter!

167

	Fade or echo.
LOU	(*Voice in her head. In the present*) It isn't my destiny. (*Sighs*) It's so clear tonight, the air is thin. It's the full moon. It's so bright you can almost see the green of the grass. It's so late. I wish I could sleep. Perhaps if I went for a walk in the garden. Bruno! (*Whine close by*) Bruno, come boy. We'll go out. Your master is home in two days, did you know that? We miss him, don't we? Come. *Footsteps as she crosses room. Opens door. Crosses hallway and opens front door. Owl hoots. In the distance a fox barks.*
LOU	(*A long sigh*) Ah! Let's be with the creatures of the night. Heel! You're not to chase after wild friends. *Rustling through undergrowth.*
LOU	What odd shapes the bushes make. *Low growl.*
LOU	Sh Bruno! Quiet. *Louder growl. Barking.*
LOU	Bad boy. Be quiet! (*Gasps*) Oh!
FRIEDA	Hello! Here Bruno, come on, good boy you know me. *Bruno whines.*
LOU	What are you doing here?
FRIEDA	Thinking.
LOU	(*Trembling with anger*) How dare you come to my house at night. How dare you disturb my peace like this! Get out!
FRIEDA	Lou, I'm sorry. I haven't been able to sleep. Things just go round in my head. I haven't slept for days. The dreams I told you, I made them up. I don't dream. I don't sleep. I can't. I'm just drawn here. Nowhere else is real.
LOU	Get out of here, I said!
FRIEDA	You have to listen to me! You must!
LOU	Our contract is ended.
FRIEDA	If I go now, I won't sleep. I could talk now, here, properly. I get confined in there, can't tell you any-

168

	thing. Tomorrow will be the same.
LOU	I said our contract is ended. I can't see you any more. It's pointless. You do nothing but tell me lies. I shall write to your husband giving him the name of a reliable colleague who will be more use to you than I am.
FRIEDA	You can't do this to me.
LOU	I'm not going to discuss it. If your husband, who, after all, persuaded you to seek treatment, wishes to talk to me, he may make an appointment.
FRIEDA	My husband! He knows nothing about me. Nothing! He understands nothing. You can't deal with me through my husband.
LOU	I've finished dealing with you.
FRIEDA	(*Laughs bitterly*) So this is the calm doctor, the wise, strong woman they've all talked about. You're a fraud, Lou Andreas Salomé, a fraud! You're weak, you can't stand pain. You protect yourself all the time.
LOU	(*Stung*) Don't be stupid! A professional relationship . . .
FRIEDA	I know, I know, I know. A professional relationship gives you the excuse to hear the pain and be untouched. I want to touch, I have to touch.
LOU	My colleague Herr . . .
FRIEDA	For God's sake, Lou! I don't need a man, I need a woman. You haven't let yourself be a woman for me, perhaps for anyone. Please, please talk to me with women's words. I'll go away, never come back, but give me of yourself, now, here. I feel I'm dying Lou. I have so much inside but no will to release what is destroying me. Help me!
	Silence. Wind stirs trees gently.
FRIEDA	(*Despairing*) You can't! You're as helpless as I am. I know you have the words somewhere inside, but you've forgotten them. You can't talk to me because you've learnt men's language. And you know that won't do! (*Begins to cry*) What

169

happened to the women in your life? Where did they go? Why didn't you listen to them? (*Stops crying*) I'll go. You're right. I won't come back.
Sound of her moving away through the bushes. She stops. Voice more distant.

FRIEDA After all, perhaps I just needed love. Goodbye, (*Emphasises last words*) Frau Andreas!
BRUNO *gives a yelping bark. Sound of garden gate opening and closing.*
LOU, *her voice trembling, begins to sing a Russian lullaby. She falters, begins to sob. Fade down.*

SCENE 17

Six weeks later.

LOU   (*Reads*) Dear Anna, Thank you for your kind
enquiries. I'm sorry that you haven't heard from
me for so long. I was confined to bed for two
weeks with a high fever and when I began to
recover I hadn't the strength to write letters. I was
in good hands. Andreas has cared for me like a
mother. I shall begin to see my patients again next
week. I have really been too unfit until now. Rainer
was desperate to visit when he heard from friends
how poorly I was. I thought it better that he should
stay away. He is so unstable for a sick room! Tell
your father I haven't had time to read his long
account of what promises to be a most interesting
case. I'll give it my attention when my eyes hurt
less. By the way, he may be interested to know that
my painter, the woman with the paralysed hand, is
apparently better. I heard from a mutual acquaint-
ance the other day. And she is preparing her
exhibition. They tell me also she is pregnant. A
strange woman. I wish her well. I must sleep now.
Take care, dear Anna. All my love, Lou.